✦

WAY OPENS:
A Spiritual Journey

✦

by Patricia Wild

b 12/44

52 Anne Spencer
Harlem RNNSNCE POET

Way Opens: A Spiritual Journey

© 2008

Patricia Wild

ISBN: 978-0-9801315-2-9

Cover Design: William J. Kelle
Cover photo used by permission of *The News and Advance*.

Warwick House Publishers
720 Court Street
Lynchburg, VA 24504

For Lynda and Owen

Permissions

14th day, 5th month. Was at Camp Creek Monthly Meeting and then rode to the mountains up James River and had a meeting at a Friend's house, in both which I felt sorrow of heart, and my tears were poured out before the Lord, who pleased to afford a degree of strength by which way opened to clear my mind amongst Friends in those places.

—A 1757 journal entry by John Woolman,
a Quaker abolitionist, as he traveled
through Virginia to meet and to pray
with slave-owning Quakers

Contents

Maybe
by Mary Oliver

Sweet Jesus, talking
    his melancholy madness,
        stood up in the boat
            and the sea lay down,

silky and sorry.
    So everybody was saved
        that night.
            But you know how it is

when something
    different crosses
        the threshold—the uncles
            mutter together,

the women walk away,
    the young brother begins
        to sharpen his knife.
            Nobody knows what the soul is.

It comes and goes
    like the wind over the water—
        sometimes, for days,
            you don't think of it.

Maybe, after the sermon,
    after the multitude was fed,
        one or two of them felt
            the soul slip forth

like a tremor of pure sunlight,
    before exhaustion,
        that wants to swallow everything,
            gripped their bones and left them

miserable and sleepy,
  as they are now, forgetting
    how the wind tore at the sails
      before he rose and talked to it—

tender and luminous and demanding
  as he always was—
    a thousand times more frightening
      than the killer sea.

Reprinted by permission.

PROLOGUE
"Sometimes, for days, you don't think of it."

Christmas week, Jamaica, 2004

Soon after the tropical sun had set, while traveling along Jamaica's northern coast on the A1, our van suddenly stopped. Before us stretched a single line of car lights; no traffic approached from the opposite direction. The eight of us, headed for a family Christmas in Ochos Rios, looked at one another. "An accident ahead," sighed Dentin, our unflappable driver, who, an hour before, had picked us up at the Montego Bay airport. A handsome, compact Jamaican in his fifties and an accountant by training, Dentin kept the van engine running so the air conditioning functioned, popped a fifties-compilation CD into the van's player, snapped on the overhead light, picked up his copy of *The Economist* from the dashboard and settled himself for a long wait. "Catch a falling star," Perry Como recommended.

Although nobly named, the A1 is, in fact, a two-lane road, unpaved in places, and, like so much of Dentin's impoverished island, wretchedly maintained. Since the moment we'd landed it had been clear that despite its distracting natural beauty, its tropical lushness, its inviting beaches and aquamarine sea, Jamaica's grinding poverty could not be ignored. Just as the cheerful, rainbow colors of the Jamaican homes and shops along the A1 could not mask their barred windows or barbed-wire fencing.

Nervously we stared out into the night. An ever-growing crowd from the small fishing village we'd just passed walked by to view the accident. From behind brightly-lit windows we observed the dark-skinned people surrounding us: teenagers dressed like mall-combing American adolescents, dreadlocked Rastafarians, older men and women, many shabbily dressed, many painfully thin: skin and bone. The villagers stared back at us. Several young men called at us through the closed windows but, unaccustomed to Jamaican patois, we could not make out what they had shouted. Dentin, I noticed, seemingly engrossed in his newspaper, clicked the van's automatic door locks.

An hour or so later, the ruby necklace of tail lights ahead of us began to slowly move. We continued along the A1 until the hotels and billboards and tacky bars of Ocho Rios. About a mile beyond the Jamaican tourist town, Dentin made a left turn. Through the sturdy, wrought-iron gate before us we spied a tennis court, a carefully tended lawn, and a brightly lit, sprawling bungalow painted a jaunty pink. We waited until the security gate creaked open and then Dentin chauffeured us to the villa's front door. Waiting there to greet us, dressed in crisp white uniforms, were the rental villa's staff. Like wedding guests, each member of our family politely shook hands with the receiving line: A young, sweet-faced Raymond. Grandmotherly Novella. Nancy with the elaborately-braided hair. Derrick the groundskeeper. Madge the cook, a faded baseball cap covering her hair. "We waited for you before serving," Raymond informed us.

The last person to arrive for dinner, I took the remaining seat at the head of a long table located on the villa's veranda. Elegantly set for twelve—four family members had arrived the day before—the table was covered with a colorful, flowery tablecloth with matching fabric napkins and graced by the soft light of candles in hurricane lamps, sparkling wine goblets, and hibiscus blossoms artfully scattered here and there.

"White or red?" Raymond asked at my elbow, holding two wine bottles. "Red," I automatically replied. (The following evening, remembering my preference, Raymond simply poured.)

Sipping my wine, I looked out at the swimming pool just feet away and the steep steps which led down to the ocean. Bats darted through the darkness, tropical insects buzzed and whirred. From where I sat I could easily hear hearty waves crash against the rocky shoreline several hundred feet below. From the kitchen, which opened onto the veranda, I heard whispers and giggles from the staff.

I've lived this scene before, I thought. I remember these candles, the delicate flower blossoms, this sultry breeze, the whispers from the kitchen.

"To Paul," I said aloud, raising my wine glass in honor of our eighty-eight-year-old host, my father-in-law, seated at the opposite end of the long, richly appointed table. For it had been his generosity that made this family Christmas in Jamaica possible.

"To Paul," everyone joined in.

For the remainder of my first evening on that tropical island, I couldn't quite shake the eerie sensation that I had uncovered a long-buried memory. Mulling over this "odd sort of memory" in my journal later that night, I decided that exhaustion and wine had no doubt enhanced my sense of so-called remembering. But with the clarity I sometimes experience during Quaker meeting, I also understood that my fatigue and those few sips of wine—on an empty stomach—had allowed a truth to reach my Inward Ear, words as clear, as audible as the whispers from the white-uniformed Jamaicans bustling in the villa's kitchen.

I remembered that White men and women eat and laugh, lit by soft candlelight, while dark-skinned people cook White people's food and serve them wine. The faces of those shabbily dressed villagers at the accident site still fresh in my mind, I remembered that every day, faceless and nameless dark-skinned people labor for me and my family, as dark-skinned people have been doing for generations.

I am White, I remembered. And unspeakably privileged.

Christmas morning, a steady wind churned the sea as most of my family snorkeled off the villa's private dock. At times I could see the others' fins, flashes of their bathing suits or trails of frothy bubbles in their wake, but for most of my time beneath the waves I was utterly alone to experience the underwater marvels of coral, iridescent fish darting below me, swaying fronds of ocean vegetation, volcanic rock formations, the quirky, undulating sand patterns on the ocean floor. A sunlit, blue-green surface riffling above my head, I listened to my steady breathing through a black plastic tube; I was one with all I viewed through my mask, completely, blissfully, serenely at peace, imbued with love for all of Spirit's creation.

On the plane going home, I learned what much of the world already knew: that an overpowering tsunami in Southeastern Asia had swept over beaches, villages, entire islands; that thousands of people had drowned, thousands had been left homeless, thousands were lost, thousands of children were now orphans. In the days that followed, as the giant waves' horrifying devastation became better and better understood, the glow of that blissful Christmas morning under water faded as quickly as my tan. Like the rest of the world, I struggled to make meaning from so much loss, so much destruction.

"How can you love a God who made tectonic plates?" one scientifically-minded member of my Quaker meeting asked with tears in his eyes.

How to make meaning that the same bucolic ocean of Christmas morning could become "the killer sea"? How to make meaning of a world which, without my lifting a finger, grants me the privileges of my race?

On a bitterly cold January night a few weeks later, I attended a benefit concert for the tsunami victims at Boston's historic Arlington Street Church. Before the concert began, the church's minister, Reverend Kim K. Crawford Harvie, spoke of the tidal disaster halfway around the world:

"If you are feeling overwhelmed," the blonde clergywoman counseled from her lofty pulpit, "you are not alone. If you are feeling powerless, you are not alone."

Overwhelmed; yes, precisely, I thought. Powerless? Why, that's exactly what I feel! How comforting, how clarifying, how surprisingly helpful to hear those words so authoritatively, yet so accurately spoken aloud.

You are not alone: I looked around me at the predominantly White audience in that drafty church. Each small group sharing one of Arlington Street's boxed pews huddled together as much for warmth as because it was a sold-out concert. Dressed, as I was, in L. L. Bean garb, somber woolen scarves wound around our necks, we squeezed together in dory-sized pews. Powerless in this world of tectonic plates, overwhelmed by a world which favors a few, relieved to be offered words with which to begin to make meaning of our experiences; we were in the same boat.

NOTES: "Sometimes for days, you don't think of it."

p. x. Quakers and drinking:
    In the 1985 *Faith and Practice of New England Yearly Meeting of Friends*, Quakers are reminded:
    "In view of the evils arising from the use of tobacco and intoxicating drinks and from the abuse of drugs, Friends are advised to consider whether they should refrain from using them, from offering them to others, and from having any share in their manufacture or sale. We should not let the claims of good fellowship or the fear of seeming peculiar influence our decision." (The Advices, p. 207)
    Although alcoholism is prevalent in my family, I nevertheless occasionally drink a glass of wine at dinner as do many of my Quaker friends.

p. xi. "I remembered that White men and women eat and laugh...":
    When discussing race, I have chosen to capitalize the first letter: Black, White, etc.

p. xii. Spirit/God:
    I *prefer* the word Spirit to the word God but use the word God occasionally.

p. xii. The Unitarian-Universalist Arlington Street Church was constructed between 1859 and 1861. Its Tiffany windows were installed between 1890 and 1923. (www.ascboston.org)

✦

Hands to work, hearts to God.
—*a Shaker saying*

✦

CHAPTER 1
Hands

Often, at Quaker meeting perhaps, I'll glance down to see that I have neatly folded my hands and placed them sedately on my lap. Without my willing it to do so, my left hand has sought my right, my fingers have separated and gently folded, my hands have assumed their carefully taught position on my thighs. Catching myself like this—and it happens all the time—conjures up a loud, boisterous, messy little girl, her braids half-undone, a restless child who bit her nails and who, according to my mother, never walked if she could run, a younger me who apparently had been told to Sit Still! so often that she unconsciously restrains herself to this day. I remember that spirited little girl, that younger me, with delight and with tremendous love.

But when I examine how my life has been impacted by race and by White privilege, I regard my folded hands with sadness and foreboding. My hands remind me that like any child, I was taught, molded by my elders. My folded hands remind me that I learned this prudish, Victorian, ladylike version of *proper* behavior so well that this early training still remains. What other lessons have I held on to? What other dicta from my elders have I, consciously or not, absorbed and accepted? How can I hope to even recognize something as pervasive as systemic racism, let alone be able to bring any clarity to my own life and experience?

The spirit of that young girl who ran when she could have walked urges me to continue, however. To the best of my ability, I am compelled to prayerfully write something on this daunting subject. That younger, irrepressible me knew so little about caution and nothing about humility. It is with both that I begin.

I start where so many conversations about race among White people often start, by telling of an early experience of "racial *others*." Four years before the U.S. Supreme Court

1

declared that "the doctrine of 'separate but equal' has no place," I began first grade in a gloomy, brick, public school in Stoneham, Massachusetts, a suburb of Boston. Proudly I carried my Hopalong Cassidy lunchbox onto the bus every day, a lunchbox which, no matter how hard my mother scrubbed it, smelled of soured milk. I wore plaid dresses with white collars, sturdy Buster Brown tie shoes, droopy white socks. In 1950, there were no public-school kindergarten classes in Massachusetts. Children born in the last months of 1944—I'd been born in December—were allowed to enter first grade. Although I had briefly attended nursery school, the rigors of public school were an unpleasant surprise.

One of the youngest and most developmentally immature students in my grade, I often leapt out of my seat, shouting: "I know! I know," when the teacher asked a question until commanded to sit down. Minutes later, however, I'd forget myself and leap up again. Once, I remember, I was tied to my chair, a piece of tape across my mouth. Weary of my misbehavior, the school's two first-grade teachers periodically handed me off to one another. "*You* take Patty for a month," those two women no doubt plotted over a cup of coffee and a hasty cigarette in the dark, oak-wainscoted teachers' room. Small wonder, therefore, that although many of the details of this early incident of *otherness* are very clear, the name and face of my teacher remain cloudy.

Right after lunch one day, my nameless, faceless teacher, standing in the front of the room behind her desk, told all of us to strip down to our undies. Beside her in front of the blackboard stood a tall, slender man in a tweed suit. This man, who I'd never seen before, might have been a doctor; he instructed that the first two or three rows of desks be pushed to one side or the rear of our classroom. Dutifully, we did what those adults had instructed, dutifully we cleared a space, dutifully our class walked around and around in a circle in our underwear in front of the teacher's desk, just as every month or so we dutifully crouched under our desks during a "Duck and Cover" air raid drill in case of nuclear attack.

As my nameless teacher and this tweedy man watched us, it soon became clear to me that although all of us had been asked to strip, those two adults weren't actually taking notice of the twenty-five or thirty White children before them. They were closely observing only one of us: our class's only "colored girl." I watched my teacher and that man whisper together about her. I understood, without anyone explaining this to me, that this stripping-down had been carefully devised so as not to single out that little girl.

Sometimes when I recall this nasty scene I want to deny it actually happened. Just writing *strip* and *undies* and *teacher* in one sentence, a voice inside me shrieks, "It must have been a dream!" Or I want to dismiss that childhood incident as a "planted" childhood memory, the kind where zealous investigators or parents or other well-meaning but inexperienced adults, by their clumsy, inept questions, create horrific recollections in the minds of children which later prove to have never actually happened.

But like the most profound myth or parable, this nasty scene feels all-too-true. Typical of a particular time and a place in American history, that incident contains layer upon layer which illustrate so much about the story of race in this country.

There are two classic authority figures, a teacher *and* a doctor, who convince thirty or so children to take off their clothing and parade around a public school classroom without question. Their authority sanctions what happened. That these authority figures stood in front of a typical fifties classroom imbue this sorry, tragic tale with a flavor as genuinely American as the unfinished Gilbert Stuart portrait of George Washington on the wall behind them or the gold-fringed American flag nearby. There's the pigtailed African American girl who, up to that afternoon, I'd taken little or no notice of but who suddenly, because of those adults' stares and whispers, became someone to fear. There's the uneasiness, the queasiness, the sexual tension of children parading in a public school classroom in their underwear. There's an apparent yet pathetic attempt to not overtly discriminate, to not consciously single out that little girl but doing so anyway. There's the deafening silence around the whole incident. There's confusion and fear and the long-reaching shadow of oppression.

3

How could I have made meaning of that incident? What experience, what language did I possess in 1950 that would help to shed light on that murky scene? Did I, for example, understand that there was a connection between my dark-skinned classmate and the appalling "Catch a Nigger by the toe" rhyme I'd learned from neighborhood children and innocently repeated to my father?

"We don't use that word," my father declared angrily. His message, however, or at least the one I absorbed, was not about oppression or prejudice but about class: People like *us* don't use that word, only ill-mannered, low-class people like those kids down the street say such things. *Trashy* people, as I would learn to say in Lynchburg, Virginia. The deeper meaning of *that word*, the stories I needed to hear, remained untold.

Consciously or not, did I associate my pigtailed classmate with those dark-skinned men who worked with my grandmother in the basement kitchen of Bridgeport, Connecticut Hospital?

My grandmother's workplace was a hellish underworld of overhead pipes, huge cauldrons of food steaming on gargantuan stoves, windowless walls made from massive, bulgy, sweaty stones and painted a vile hospital-green. Above me, I knew, loomed a many-storied building filled with sick people. In the time it took for me to acknowledge these patients' existence and to imagine their pain and suffering, someone might have just died. Warned by my grandmother to keep away from those "not nice" Black men, terrified of getting burned, I'd park myself in what seemed a safe place: on a tall stool beside the industrial-sized can opener—which smelled of tomato soup—at the end of a long, stainless steel table. Through an archway to my left I could watch those Black men, their skin shiny with sweat, dressed in white, as they pushed heavy, chromed hot-food trolleys up a steep ramp from the kitchen to the elevator. Seated on my safe perch, idly biting my nails, I saw those dark-skinned men struggle, I heard them curse under their breath. If I turned my gaze toward the other end of the kitchen I could watch my grandmother and her co-workers, red-faced, fleshy Polish women who smelled

4

of baby powder and sweat, their hair in unbecoming nets, stir bubbling pots. Sitting in that steamy kitchen, did I connect the childhood Who's It? rhyme and my pigtailed classmate and the cursing men?

It was only as an adult that I understood that one of the few jobs open to those struggling men, the limited-English Poles, or to my finishing school–educated grandmother had been the hot, grueling work in Bridgeport Hospital's kitchen. After divorcing her equally privileged husband, my grandmother had to support herself and her two young daughters, one of them my mother. Taught how to pour tea but not much else at her elite school, my grandmother's career choices were as prescribed as were those of her fellow kitchen workers. As difficult as her job had been, however, my grandmother always knew she could draw upon her family's money and resources, a safety net woven by generations of well-to-do ancestors. Just as I, faced with a divorce of my own, understood that my daughters and I were supported by that same net.

Another image: Unlike the other little girls in our first-grade class, my African American classmate wasn't wearing an undershirt. I can still picture her mahogany body against the whiteness of her panties. In my white cotton underpants and sleeveless, white cotton undershirt with its tiny, white bow on the front, I recognized both that something was profoundly wrong and that I was required to ignore my queasy feelings. At age five, although still struggling to sit still and to fold my hands, I had already learned to shut down, to accept.

✦

It is late fall on a bleak Thursday afternoon in Syracuse, New York. The maple trees outside my piano teacher's house have already lost their leaves and the battleship-gray clouds above them portend snow. I am twelve, far too young to anticipate that some day, when telling stories of my childhood, my piano teacher's name, Mrs. Mulfinger, will become a delightful detail. Just as I am far too young to understand that Mrs.

Mulfinger's frequent and heavy sighs don't *necessarily* signify her profound disappointment with how I play the piano but might be an early sign of emphysema.

I sit in Mrs. Mulfinger's frumpy living room reading a *Reader's Digest*. In the nearby sunporch, my best friend, Linda Lloyd-Jones, has her lesson. Linda and I have received permission to leave our suburban junior high early every Thursday afternoon so that we can catch the bus into Syracuse for our lessons. I can hear Linda's flawless performance through the sunporch's French door. Linda is already a couple of piano books ahead of me even though she hardly seems to practice. Biting my nails, I select another *Reader's Digest* from the pile beside Mrs. Mulfinger's couch.

I read a gruesome, true-life story about a cruel Nazi jailer, a woman, who forces a cowering prisoner to drink his own urine. Or perhaps I read a survivor's gruesome account of Dachau. In the mid-fifties, the *Reader's Digest* often contained such Holocaust material. While I read, Mrs. Mulfinger's dachshund frantically licks my leg and Linda plays "Fur Elise" with few mistakes. The dog licks, licks, licks. Horrified by what I read, I am only dimly aware of the small, warm creature poised beside my outstretched legs. From time to time I brusquely push the panting dog away. Relentless, she returns to lick, lick, lick. Much as I long to kick or slap Mrs. Mulfinger's annoying pet, I cannot, will not. And curling my legs under me, hiding them under my skirt to protect myself from that tongue is not an option. The same child told not to say "Nigger," the same little girl trained to fold her hands neatly in her lap, would never put her shoes on her piano teacher's upholstery. Too polite to even turn on a light in the darkening room, I keep reading.

✦

Stiffly I pose, seated at a Kranich and Bach baby grand. A wedding gift to my beloved paternal grandmother, the curly-mahogany piano is now mine. A few feet away, Carolyn Gorton Fuller, a gangly Virginian who has been hired by my mother, struggles with my portrait. I am fifteen years old. Carolyn, her easel, the piano, a couch and accompanying coffee table, a couple of arm chairs, several lamps, a stereo and speakers, an overflowing bookcase or two and I are jumbled together in the front room of a pokey rented house on Peakland Place, one of Lynchburg, Virginia's, loveliest residential streets. Over Carolyn's shoulder, through the windows behind her, I can see the dogwoods planted along Peakland Place's median strip in full bloom. This is our family's first, astonishingly beautiful spring in Lynchburg, week after week of soft, gentle breezes and a lushness none of us, born and raised in the North, have ever experienced.

Our family and six-hundred *other* General Electric Company-affiliated families now live in this central-Virginia city because GE, wishing to avoid northern labor unions, has transferred one of its divisions here. Located south of Charlottesville, near the Blue Ridge mountains and beside the James River, Lynchburg numbers about fifty-five thousand residents, a third of them African American.

Years later, long after the Cold War had ended, my father described his work while we lived in Lynchburg: "I was a merchant of death... Moving involved a raise. With four children, it was important to keep an increasing flow of money."

How much was my 1982 decision to become a Quaker rooted in my resentment that our family had been so abruptly uprooted in 1959? Can I separate my adolescent rage and powerlessness from my fierce joy, many years later, to discover how deeply George Fox's words: "We utterly deny all outward wars and strife and fightings with outward weapons, for any end or under any pretense whatsoever" moved me?

The six of us are jammed together in this two-bedroom apartment—the dining room has been converted into a third bedroom—while our new house is being designed. My parents have bought a wedge-shaped piece of land a little further out from Peakland Place. While the architect they hired finalizes his plans, the Wild family impatiently waits in this cheek by jowl apartment.

I vividly remember the rainy, Saturday afternoon when my parents realized they had to make other living arrange-

7

ments. For reasons I don't remember, I accompanied my mother and father when they met with their architect at his downtown office. The elevator serving his multi-story office building was operated by a young, uniformed girl, a "Negra" as they said in Lynchburg. While my parents and the architect conferred, I sat in the waiting room until, bored, I walked to the elevator and pushed the button.

"Hi," I said when the elevator girl—let's call her Wanda— opened the door. "What's at the top of this building?"

Because it was a Saturday, Wanda was as bored as I. Up to the top floor we zoomed, down to the lobby. As much as I begged, Wanda would not let me take over the controls. Once she stopped the elevator between floors and, silent, we imagined the steely shaft of air above and below us. After we'd taken several trips up and down together, Wanda pushed the "B" button and our tiny craft sped down, down, until, with a couple of jolts, we stopped and Wanda opened the folding brass cage and then the elevator door.

Although by age fifteen I'd spent plenty of time in the basement of Bridgeport Hospital, the scene just outside the elevator was nothing I could have anticipated. Yes, there were the same pipes running along the ceiling, the same dank walls, the same dimmed light from grimy basement windows. Instead of stoves and stainless steel tables, however, the room before me was dominated by a gigantic boiler around which clustered maybe fifteen or twenty Black people of all ages. Laundry lines hung from the boiler, families were eating, there was laughter, children running under foot; I stared.

An older Black man stepped forward from the crowd. "She doesn't belong here," he said to Wanda, sternly. "Take her back."

Without speaking, without saying goodbye, Wanda delivered me to the architect's floor and I glumly returned to the waiting room.

Like so much of what I'd observed in Lynchburg, I didn't know how to make meaning of that basement scene. Instinctively I sensed that those dark-skinned families and their drying laundry were not supposed to be huddled around that boiler. So when my furious parents emerged from the architect's inner office, having just fired him, I said nothing of what I saw.

How to make meaning of segregated Lynchburg, Virginia, in 1959? How to make meaning of the disturbing changes in my own family since we arrived? My brother, Paul, two years younger than I, normally ebullient, has been strangely quiet. "I felt like I didn't say a word for an entire year and no one noticed," Paul said later.

When we first arrived in Lynchburg, my mother coped in her usual capable way. Adept at assessing any new community's culture from having moved several times before, in short order she enrolled my brothers and sister in Lynchburg's best public schools—there is only one choice for high school-aged me—and my sister Deborah in Floyd Ward Dancing School, where Lynchburg's elite send their children to plié and to curtsey. She and my father bought land in an up-and-coming neighborhood, joined the more prestigious of Lynchburg's two country clubs, learned how to play golf and, some might say, in a painfully obvious attempt to be accepted socially, hired Carolyn Gorton Fuller to paint her children's portraits. But when my father went away on one of his many business trips, my mother stayed in bed. Some mornings it was up to me to get everyone dressed, fed, and out the door for school. How to make meaning of the changes in my parents?

"I can't get your eyes right," Carolyn Gorton Fuller complains. "Could you please sit still?"

The Lynchburg painter captured thirteen-year-old Paul's haunting sweetness and seven-year-old Deborah's frenetic energy on canvas and produced such a winsome portrait of five-year-old Benjy in his navy-blue sailor's suit that when Ms. Fuller later exhibited her work, it received great Lynchburg acclaim. But indeed, the society painter did not get my eyes, nor much else of me, right.

These days, I choose to walk instead of run. My sixty-three-year-old body begins to surprise me with what it can no longer do or, just as startling, what it does without my bidding. So recently, when I came upon that portrait carelessly stored in my attic, it was easy to forgive Ms. Fuller for my crooked eyes, that too-long neck, how she had painted my hair as if cemented onto my head. For the Lynchburg artist did depict one tiny detail of the adolescent me with skill and charm: My baby finger. That same pinky which always refused to curl nicely over Mrs. Mulfinger's piano keys but instead, much as I willed it otherwise, pointed straight up in the air, harbinger of future bodily betrayals.

✦

Over my desk hangs a Picasso print of a pensive young mother and her nursing baby. To the side and below the figures of the mother and child, Picasso had charcoaled a preliminary outline of the mother's head, neck and shoulders, and five studies, one of them just a few strokes, of the mother's long-fingered, elegant hands. This same print had hung in my room at Pendle Hill, a Quaker retreat center near Pennsylvania's Swarthmore College. In the summer of 1984, novelist Daisy Newman and I led a creative writing workshop at Pendle Hill. When the week-long workshop ended, I'd bought my own copy of Picasso's sketch. As I write, now, I sometimes glance at that print, an ever-present reminder that even great artists like Picasso are sometimes tentative, cautious. The print is also a souvenir of my extraordinary week with Daisy Newman.

A member of Friends Meeting at Cambridge and a highly regarded Quaker writer, Daisy Newman took me and three other women writers under her wing soon after I'd begun attending Friends Meeting. Every few months or so, having secured a babysitter for my daughters, I'd ride with one of those writers, Wendy Sanford, to Daisy's house in tony, country-chic Lincoln. At the time of these visits, Wendy, a member of the Boston Women's Health Book Collective, was writing for and editing *Our Bodies, Ourselves*.

"I hope we can have a good, long grace today," Wendy said one morning as we cruised along Route 2. "I really need some time to worship."

A Quaker grace, which my daughters call "Hands," is a period of silence before a meal when diners hold hands and pray, give thanks, bless the food and the people gathered at the table. After a few moments, someone squeezes a hand, the signal to begin eating.

When she and I arrived at Daisy's lovely home, Wendy shared her hope with our hostess. After we'd gathered around Daisy's glass table, our brown-bag lunches before us, the five of us, heads bowed, held hands. Almost immediately Daisy squeezed my hand. Startled, I looked up. Daisy, at her usual place at the end of the table, grinned at all of us. "I'm hungry," she explained.

Those brown-bag lunches at Daisy's were, in fact, a series of lectures by our hostess about her writing process. Her own daughter a medical doctor, Daisy regarded us as her writing daughters, her *Quaker* writing daughters, to whom she wished to impart her stories. She told us, for example, how she brought her characters to meeting for worship every Sunday, how she would listen to what the fictitious Oliver and Loveday and red-headed Serenity whispered to her Inward Ear.

The first time I experienced a Quaker meeting, in 1965, it was Daisy Newman who greeted me—and my Sunday school class—at the door. A junior at Wheelock College and in need of extra cash, I'd taken a job teaching a Unitarian-Universalist high school class at the Second Church in Boston. My eight students called themselves the Scibs, after their church's initials. In 1965, Second Church was located on the corner of Beacon and Park streets, walking distance from Wheelock's Riverway campus. Using *The Church Across the Street* as our guide, the Scibs and I traipsed all over greater-Boston attending services at, perhaps, the Christian Science Mother Church one Sunday or a Catholic mass in the North End on another. I found these spiritual explorations as fascinating as my teenaged class did. But for very different reasons.

Like my Sunday school students, I, too, had been raised Unitarian-Universalist. Unlike them, however, as an adolescent, I'd attended a Unitarian church in Bible-belt Lynchburg, where the second question, after asking a new person's name, was usually: "What church do you go to?" In a southern city dominated by Baptists and Episcopalians, being a teenaged

Unitarian simply amplified my already-established oddity. "Unitarian? That some kind of Yankee religion?" For the Scibs, however, living in a region where being a Unitarian-Universalist was hardly unusual, their Protestant affiliation was a source of enormous pride. A visit to a Catholic or a Christian Science church simply reinforced what those teenagers already believed: to be a U-U was to be superior. And while I generally agreed with that opinion, especially having endured the disdain and puzzlement of my Lynchburg peers, theologically, there were aspects of my sect I found disquieting. Especially at Easter.

One spring morning when I was about ten, for example, I went up the street to Linda Lloyd-Jones's house. The living room shades were drawn and when Linda greeted me at the front door, she spoke in hushed tones.

"What's the matter?" I stared at her round face; her eyes were red. "Have you been crying?"

My best friend who, like the rest of her family, was Catholic, looked at me sorrowfully. "It's Good Friday," Linda reminded me. "The day Christ died on the cross," she added for good measure. "It's a very sad day for us. So I can't come out to play." Gently she closed the door.

Walking home I mulled over Linda's grief-stricken eyes, her house's drawn shades. The crucifixion had a very real and painful meaning for the Lloyd-Jones family, I realized. How could I breezily dismiss the Easter story as a *metaphor* after visiting Linda's house? Neatly categorizing the events surrounding the crucifixion and resurrection as a "renewal and rebirth tale," as I'd been taught in Unitarian Sunday school, denied something I saw in my best friend's brown eyes, something powerful, something inexplicable, something beyond words, something that I suddenly discovered I longed for.

"We don't know what happened at Easter," someone at Cambridge Meeting once said years later. "But we do know this: There is mystery."

Yes, I thought. That one word perfectly sums it up for me; it's all I need.

To attend our very first Quaker meeting, the Scibs and I took the subway to Harvard Square, arriving at the Quaker meeting house off Brattle Street a little late. Noisy and irrepressible, the adolescent Scibs and their scarcely older teacher burst through the doors. Standing by the meeting house entrance was an older woman, her gray hair cut in a no-nonsense style, wearing a navy blue sweater and matching skirt, and sensible shoes. Daisy, I remember, shushed us; chastened, we slunk up the stairs to the balcony.

As we and the hundred or so people in that meeting house settled into worship, I began to understand "the helpfulness of silence." On a Sunday morning at church when a U-U minister instructed, "Let us pray," I would have been allowed a few precious seconds of silence before a spoken-aloud prayer was delivered from the pulpit. Those few seconds had never been enough for me. But here in this simple, unadorned meeting house, I saw that I'd be able to pray, muse, contemplate for more than a few, scant moments. So although Friends Meeting at Cambridge is noted for its "popcorn" meetings, the silence that Sunday morning in 1965 was for me ample, rich, delicious. A few weeks later, my father remembers, during a Father-Daughter Weekend at Wheelock, I brought my father to Cambridge Meeting, eager to share a Quaker meeting with this "merchant of death." Many years, three marriages, four children and two stepchildren later, Friends Meeting at Cambridge has become my spiritual home.

I sit on a facing bench at Quaker meeting now, beside my husband, my hands neatly folded, and gaze across to the next bench where Daisy always sat. For several months after she died, although every Sunday brings newcomers to Quaker worship in that meeting house, no one, not even the many strangers among us, took Daisy's place. No one could.

NOTES: Hands

p. 1. "[R]acial *others*" is a term used by Tim Wise in his *White Like Me*:

"Whites too often believe we are not experiencing race until someone who isn't white is in the room we're in, ignoring the inconvenient truth that the whiteness of whatever room we're in didn't just happen." (p. 9)

p. 2. In 1950, blackboards actually *were* black.

p. 2. "Nuclear attack"

My parents were so terrified that the Russians would launch a missile from Boston Harbor that in 1952 our family moved a few miles inland to Stow, Massachusetts.

p. 4. "...someone might have just died."

My grandmother, who wanted to be called Lil, lived close to Bridgeport Hospital. When we visited her, I'd lie awake in her bedroom made distressingly dark by the World War II blackout shades still on her windows and, terrified, listen to the nightly sounds of ambulances racing to the hospital. Thoughts of suffering and death were very much a part of my trips to Lil's house.

p. 6. Linda and I attended Fayetteville-Manlius Junior High and lived on Lakeview Drive, a dead-end street lined with thirteen houses built, in the early fifties, on former farmland. Many of the Lakeview Drive fathers, including Linda's and mine, worked at GE's Electronics Park.

p. 7. "merchant of death"

Like so many of the costly expenditures of the Cold War, the communications systems my father, sales manager of GE's military sales, sold to this country's armed forces to be used should the Russians attack, were never employed.

p. 11. *The Church Across the Street*

Written by Reginald D. Manwell and Sophia Lyon Fahs and first published by the Beacon Press in 1947, this book, like so many U-U books created for Sunday school students, is well-written, accessible, and highly informative.

p. 12. The Lloyd-Jones's Catholicism

Linda's mother, Rose, was Hungarian. Only as an adult did I consider what Rose's faith might have meant to her in light of the fact that, when the Lloyd-Jones and the Wilds had lived on Lakeview Drive, Hungary had been under the control of "Godless Communists."

p. 13. "The helpfulness of silence in group worship and fellowship is one of the greatest lessons the Society of Friends has demonstrated."
From *The Church Across the Street* section on the Society of Friends, p. 170 (1958 edition).

p. 13. "popcorn" meetings

When one and then another and then another person rises to speak.

p. 13. Father-Daughter Weekends

Like most colleges and universities these days, Wheelock now hosts *Parents'* Weekends.

◆

Those Winter Sundays
by Robert Hayden

Sundays too my father got up early
and put his clothes on in the blueblack cold,
then with cracked hands that ached
from labor in the weekday weather made
banked fires blaze. No one ever thanked him.

I'd wake and hear the cold splintering, breaking.
When the rooms were warm, he'd call,
and slowly I would rise and dress,
fearing the chronic angers of that house,

speaking indifferently to him,
who had driven out the cold
and polished my good shoes as well.
What did I know, what did I know
of love's austere and lonely offices?

◆

Reprinted by permission.

CHAPTER 2
"What did I know, what did I know?"

Winter mornings in Fayetteville, I'd lie in bed listening to the tinkling sound of my mother's silver belt buckle as she began that day's chores. A multi-tasker before the word had been invented, my bustling mother always completed dressing on the run, threading her belt through her pants loops while gathering that day's laundry. My nose red with cold—we always slept with our windows open—I snuggled under my thick quilt and waited: Would my mother approach my chilly bedroom to rouse me for school? Or was it, as I fervently hoped, a snow day? If so, my efficiency-expert mother, a basket of laundry on her hip, bypassed my room and proceeded directly down the stairs to fix breakfast for my father.

So, in the early hours of Sunday, January 28, 1962, when a freakish snowstorm dumped almost a foot of snow on Lynchburg, our family reacted almost with relief. So much of Lynchburg, Virginia, bewildered or depressed us. But snow? We knew snow.

"This'll melt by noontime," my father, who turned forty-seven that day, confidently predicted. Nevertheless, my parents decided to forego church. Lynchburg's Unitarian church, a tiny, lovely stone structure perched midway up downtown's steep hill and only accessible by staircase, was attended by a handful of parishioners, many of them fellow Yankee transplants. My parents, my father in particular, felt strongly that our family had a responsibility to consistently show up. But in his mind, the precipitous and unplowed streets of Lynchburg and snow-ignorant drivers posed too much of a threat. The Wilds would stay at what was now home, a boxy, roomy, split-level just off Peakland Place.

Foregoing church also meant foregoing the Hotel Virginian for a birthday dinner for my father. A short walk from church, down the Monument Terrace staircase to the corner of Church and Eighth streets, the Hotel Virginian was our favorite place for Sunday dinner. The hotel's genteelly shabby dining room, the African American string quartet softly playing in one corner, its traditional fare, and scarcity of diners—we sometimes had the dining room to ourselves—allowed the six of us to relax in an atmosphere both Southern, yet accessible. Going to the Hotel Virginian after church and always ordering chocolate parfaits for dessert became a family tradition. Strangers in a strange land, the Wilds were as hungry for tradition and for ritual as we were for the hotel's tasty beaten biscuits.

Dressed in our church clothes and seated around our favorite round table, serenaded by the dining room's Black, tuxedoed musicians playing something by Strauss, perhaps, my family knew we looked good; our pervading sense of alienation made us intensely self-conscious as if constantly watching ourselves in a large mirror. "Wouldn't this make a great picture?" my brother, Paul, often asked on family outings.

Yes it would: There sits Al Wild, successful executive with General Electric, a tall, handsome man whose well-tailored suit minimizes the considerable weight he's gained since marriage.

Beside him is my mother, Pat, nearly as tall as her husband, a stunning woman whose keen blue eyes search out table-manners transgressions on the part of her four children. After her initial depression when we'd first arrived, my mother has regained her considerable energy. Recently, in addition to civic activities, a busy social life, and playing golf, she has begun classes at Randolph-Macon Woman's College.

Paul, at age fourteen, is still pubescent; after three years in Lynchburg, his sweet, boyish face retains the deer-in-the-headlights bewilderment that, for reasons he cannot understand, he and the rest of us live here.

Deborah, age nine, is blonde and sturdy; she wears a white-collared, smocked dress and, as she has done since she was three, glasses. Determined to hold her own as the third oldest, Debby has recently memorized a series of joke books and, no matter what topic may come up at dinner, can deliver two or three appropriate jokes, some of them actually funny.

Benjamin, age seven, has outgrown his natty sailor outfit and now wears a suit like his father and older brother. Wide-eyed, curious, Benjy studies the Hotel Virginian dining room. Of all of us, only Benjy actually acknowledges—and wonders about—those well-dressed, dark-skinned men just feet away from where we eat.

At seventeen, I am a teenaged version of my mother; we even share the same name—although I am now known as "Pepper." "Patty" until I was ten, I'd acquired my new name at a Girl Scout camp on Cape Cod. That fall when our family moved to Fayetteville, I'd told Linda Lloyd-Jones that my name was Pepper; she and the other fifth-graders believed me. In Lynchburg, where family names are often first names, my puerile name rarely merits comment.

Because of the snowstorm, however, there would be no Hotel Virginian dinner that cold, late-January Sunday. Instead, my mother made pancakes and we settled for a cozy day inside.

"Can I stay in my pajamas all day?" Debby, always testing parental limits, requested.

"Why not," my father answered.

I spent the afternoon sledding with friends and went to bed that night hoping for a snow day but awoke to everyday weekday sounds.

Which meant I had a problem: What would I use for a coat on such a wintry day? The week before, when driving back to Lynchburg after a week's skiing near Pittsburgh, I'd carelessly left my warm woolen coat in a restaurant in Pennsylvania. Although my father always provided Paul and me with door-to-door service, his Buick convertible's heater didn't really begin to function until *after* he'd dropped us off at E. C. Glass. "The car got nice and warm right after you two left," he'd tease us at dinner. What to wear?

An unexpected snowstorm and the petty, trifling concern over a missing coat; these I clearly remember over forty years later. What I cannot remember is any conversation or discussion of what was about to happen on January 29, 1962. Everyone in Lynchburg knew what was about to happen. For weeks, the two Lynchburg newspapers, both owned by the ubiquitous Glass family, had trumpeted that, like it or not, two African American students would begin classes at E. C. Glass that day. But as I recall, during the weeks leading up to that historic event, neither my family nor my U-U church community discussed the two Black students' pending arrival. Not even in the privacy of our home did my family talk about the U.S. Supreme Court's *Brown* decision, "separate but equal" schools, the Freedom Rides, segregation. "We didn't do enough," my mother says sadly, now. Like polite guests obeying Lynchburg's house rules, we kept silent.

I *can* remember—with great embarrassment—one family conversation, prompted by an early civil rights demonstration in Lynchburg in the fall of 1960. Dressed in a pastel shirt-waist dress, a matching cardigan over my shoulders, tasseled loafers from Coleman's Shoe Store, and white gloves, I'd taken the bus downtown that day to do a little shopping. Like most teenagers in my neighborhood, I received a generous allowance; I also ran a successful children's party business. So I could afford to shop for clothes at upscale Miller and Rhoads or Baldwin's department stores, buy a new silver charm for my already jangly charm bracelet at Buckingham-Flippin jewelers, then consume a coke and a packet of peanut-butter Nabs at a Main Street drug store lunch counter.

On the day I'm remembering, the usual downtown crowds were joined by ten or twelve neatly-dressed African Americans who silently walked in a circle on Main Street in front of Woolworth's Five and Ten. That evening at dinner, I proudly told my family what I'd done to "support" these silent civil rights walkers, who were protesting the store's segregated lunch counter.

"I bought a pair of sunglasses," I announced. "It was hard to find anything in that store that I wanted so I finally just bought sunglasses. With white frames. Like Jackie Kennedy wears. Only white."

My father, my Republican, anti-labor, business-executive father, slowly lowered his fork. "You crossed a picket line?" he asked incredulously, then gave my mother a look I knew well. Can you believe a daughter of ours could be so stupid? this look said.

"What's a picket line?" I asked. Only then did it occur to my parents that their teenaged daughter genuinely had no idea what she'd done. Gently, they gave me a brief lesson on the labor movement: on boycotts, picket lines, and strikes. And, of course, given their background and upbringing, my mother and father talked about feather-bedding and malingering and how labor leaders were, in their opinion, often members of the Communist Party. Did they mention that it was to avoid unions that GE had moved all of us to Lynchburg? Of course not.

What my family did not discuss that evening in 1960, and what wasn't being discussed around dining room tables all over the nation that night was the cruel injustice of Jim Crow, why sit-ins and Freedom Rides were happening, and most important, *why* people who looked like our family could sit at a drug store counter, take a seat in the front of a bus, attend well-equipped, well-maintained schools, without hesitation, without question.

On the morning of January 29, 1962, having put on a warm sweater and my ski jacket, I emerged from my father's still-frigid Buick, my brother beside me, and walked up the slushy sidewalk to school. Do I remember police cars parked in front?

Of the two of us, Paul was far more likely to actually meet and to share classes with Owen Cardwell and Lynda Woodruff, who, at fourteen and thirteen, respectively, were to begin ninth grade at Glass that day. A senior, I saw no sign of "the two Negroes" walking through Glass's commodious hallways that morning, nor, thankfully, did I see any attendant violence.

It was at lunch that day that I first saw Owen Cardwell, tall and thin, just as he emerged from the food-serving area and, carrying a laden tray, walked slowly toward the cafeteria's long tables. The way I remember it, Owen approached one table and the two or three boys who'd been sitting there immediately jumped up and moved away. Owen sat down to eat alone.

Yankee transplant, sneered at for being "tacky," I knew what it felt like to be a reviled and despised outsider. From

21

Mrs. Mulfinger's *Reader's Digest*, I knew what had happened when German citizens remained silent in the face of Hitler's oppression. Indeed, sitting in my piano teacher's living room, I'd always imagined that if the Nazis came to *my* German village, I'd bravely do whatever was necessary to protect my Jewish neighbors. I knew I was supposed to walk over to Owen's table and sit beside him. But I did not.

Thirty-seven years later, during a phone call from Lynchburg, Virginia, I told that shameful lunchtime story again. My first novel, *Swimming In It*, had just been published by the Flower Valley Press in Gaithersburg, Maryland. Like many authors working with small presses, I had discovered that much of the publicity and promotion for this fledgling novel were to be largely *my* responsibility. Because my book's red-headed protagonist, Jewell McCormick, had been born in Lynchburg, Virginia, in 1962, I'd hoped Lynchburg residents might want to read her story. So I mailed a copy to a nameless "Arts Editor" of the city's newspaper, *The News and Advance*. A couple of weeks later, Darrell Laurant, Yankee-born columnist for the Lynchburg paper, interviewed me over the phone.

In *Swimming In It,* the fictional Jewell, having been sexually abused by her mother's tenant, flees from Lynchburg at age fifteen. Most of the novel takes place in Somerville, Massachusetts, a working-class city adjacent to Boston and Cambridge and where I have lived since 1979. Why, Darrell asked me, had I chosen to have Jewell born in Lynchburg?

"I lived in Lynchburg from 1959 until 1962," I told him.

"GE?" the reporter asked.

"GE, indeed," I replied.

Like Jewell's mother, I told him, I'd attended E. C. Glass High School; several of my classmates, including five of my friends, had become pregnant our senior year. Jewell's mother's experiences as a pregnant high school student were written from my memory of those friends.

"Oh," noted Darrell, who'd written a book on Lynchburg history, "then you were at E. C. Glass when it was integrated!"

Darrell's use of the word "integrated" reminded me of a passage from *Swimming In It* when Jewell challenges her mother's use of the same word:

"How can you call that 'integration'? I [Jewell] asked. I've looked at your yearbook a hundred times. And all I ever saw was one skinny, frightened black kid tucked away in a corner somewhere."

She [Jewell's mother] looked at me like she always did: like she was contemplating hitting me hard. To my relief she merely shrugged her lovely shoulders. "All right," she admitted. "It was only a couple of negras but it was a Big Change, Jewell. I'm telling you. A Big Change."

Perhaps it was speaking to someone from Lynchburg that made me realize that the "skinny, frightened black kid tucked away in a corner somewhere" was not a fictitious character like Jewell or her mother but an actual, flesh-and-blood person. Maybe it was thirty-seven years of guilt. Or perhaps my impulse to tell my humiliating high school story to Darrell Laurant, a stranger *and* a reporter, was divinely inspired. For whatever reason, the cotton batting of obliviousness, defensiveness, denial, and inattention which usually surrounds me in matters of race was momentarily removed and I was able to be open and honest.

Yes, I told Darrell, I had indeed been at E. C. Glass that January day in 1962 when the first two African Americans entered the school. I then told Darrell Laurant my cafeteria story. "My inaction that day has been a pivotal moment in my life," I told him, only realizing as I said these words that they were indeed true.

"I can help you find Lynda Woodruff, at least," the Lynchburg reporter offered. "Lynda Woodruff's mother and stepfather still live in town." Darrell also offered to send me a copy of his book. Months later, having read Darrell Laurant's *A City Unto Itself: Lynchburg, Virginia in the 20th Century*, in which Lynda Woodruff was frequently quoted, I labored over a letter to the former "Negro desegregator" which, with trepidation, I finally mailed to her. "I hope I hear from you and understand if I don't," my March 2000 letter ended. For I knew that no matter how carefully I had tried to craft my letter, my words might irritate or anger this unknown woman. And Lynda Woodruff might very well resent being reminded of her experiences at E. C. Glass High School.

Six months later, in August of 2000, I received a letter on North Georgia College and State University stationery and a business card from Lynda Woodruff; *Dr*. Woodruff, according to her card, was a professor of physical therapy at the Dahlonega, Georgia, university.

"Over the years I have had many letters like yours," the college professor wrote, "have met people in Lynchburg who were there but didn't step forward, and have even worked with those who called me Nigger and threatened to kill us." Her letter also contained Owen Cardwell's address. I wrote to Reverend Owen Cardwell immediately.

That same summer that Dr. Woodruff's much-welcomed, revealing letter arrived, I'd been wrestling with the sequel to *Swimming In It*, entitled *Welling Up*. Emulating Daisy Newman's writing technique, I had brought my fictitious characters, Jewell McCormick and the other women from her Somerville homeless shelter, to meeting for worship every week. The resulting novel had been an easeful, Spirit-led process from the first page until the end. For *Welling Up*, however, every word, every scene, every plot turn was uphill work. At first I thought my fears about writing a second book were holding me back. For I'd heard stories from other writers how second books are often judged more harshly than the first. But one day, while working on a scene between Jewell and her mother, which took place at a posh Lynchburg country club, I noticed something. While the scene featured the two White characters, my attention, like a wayward movie camera, kept focusing on the African American men in the background: the caddies waiting in the shade of a large pecan tree near the club's parking lot, the attentive waiter—based on Boonsboro Country Club's Malcolm Jefferson—in his impeccable white uniform. Who are those Black men? I wondered, staring at my computer screen. What are their stories? Could those caddies actually support families with their earnings? Who *was* Malcolm Jefferson? Why, I wondered, were those dark-skinned men so much more compelling to write about than the fictional Jewell and her mother?

One Saturday morning in September of 2000, the phone rang; it was Reverend Owen Cardwell, "the skinny, frightened black kid tucked away in a corner somewhere." Dr. Cardwell, now a Baptist preacher in Richmond, Virginia, spoke with a deep, resonant, Virginia-flavored voice; the fourteen-year-old who'd sat alone in a high school cafeteria, the man I'd treated as though a fictitious character in my book, spoke without anger, without rancor, without bitterness. The gentleness of Reverend Cardwell's voice made me cry.

As it happened, I had picked up the phone that morning, car keys in hand. When Reverend Cardwell called, I was about to drive to Greenfield, Massachusetts, to celebrate poet Phil Sosis's eighty-sixth birthday.

Phil Sosis was my first husband's stepfather. Although technically not related to him, my daughter Melissa nevertheless considered Phil her grandfather. At Phil's party, Melissa staged a reading of an interview she'd conducted with her grandfather. Most of the party-goers knew that Phil had spent several years of his childhood in a New York City orphanage; his well-wishers knew Phil to be a gifted poet. They remembered that his résumé included union organizer and factory worker and, later in his life, teacher and vocational counselor. Melissa's staged interview—with her fiancé Dave Arons reading Phil's words—revealed one of her grandfather's lesser-known roles: as a member of Paul Robeson's honor guard at a 1949 Peekskill, New York, concert. When the African American singer, branded "Un-American" for his progressive views, had been threatened by American Legion members, courageous men like Phil Sosis surrounded the performer, shielding Robeson from possible attack or a sniper's bullet.

"I was on the stage," Dave as Phil Sosis read to the birthday party crowd. "I volunteered to give my life for him if necessary."

Many of Phil's birthday guests, it turned out, had either attended Robeson's Peekskill concert or knew people who had been there; during lunch, many people told their own stories of that infamous day in 1949.

Listening to their lunchtime stories, that morning's phone call with Reverend Cardwell very much on my mind, I was struck by how many stories, both of unspeakable oppression and of personal courage, don't get told. Like most Americans, for example, I'd known next-to-nothing about the Paul Robeson concert in Peekskill until I heard Melissa's interview with her grandfather. So many of the stories, I realized, center around African American history and Black people's day-to-day experiences.

In the quiet of Quaker meeting the next day, this growing awareness, called forth by Owen Cardwell's gentle voice and the Paul Robeson stories, deepened. As with Pirandello's play, *Six Characters in Search of an Author*, when thwarted creative expression assumes human form, stories of the African American experience pressed at me, nudged me during worship. "Tell us," they seemed to whisper.

Is this my ministry? I asked Spirit. Is this what's called "a leading?"

According to my journal, that same Sunday, *The Boston Globe* quoted a Black Muslim's condemnation of "the white devil media." (That I'd failed to note this man's name but instead labeled him tells the briefest of stories.) I read this African American man's denunciation with growing excitement. A published novelist, a columnist for the local paper, a free-lance writer for a couple of fairly prestigious publications, well-connected to other writers and film-makers, I had access to that so-called white devil media. I can *use* my Whiteness to tell these stories. "I feel so empowered," I wrote in my journal.

Two days later, I received a phone call from Friends General Conference's book-catalogue coordinator. The umbrella organization for unprogrammed meetings like Friends Meeting at Cambridge, FGC offers a number of resources to Quakers such as teaching materials, workshops, books and pamphlets, and every summer, conducts a Gathering of Friends conference for Quakers from meetings all over the country. Because *Swimming In It* hadn't sold well at that summer's Gathering, the coordinator explained, my novel would not be listed in the upcoming FGC catalogue.

Like most writers, I am no stranger to rejection. As a one-person *Swimming In It* promotion, distribution, *and* sales manager, I knew how difficult it is for a first novel, published by a tiny press and written by an unknown, to be noticed. Nevertheless, that phone call crushed me. Me! One of Daisy Newman's writing daughters! Me! So eager to launch this fledgling writing project! After a couple of tearful days, I handed over my disappointment and hurt to Spirit. Eventually it came to me that the publishing business is just that: a business. Quaker-affiliated businesses, like any business, have to pay attention to the bottom line.

While more at peace with FGC's decision, my faith in my just-begun leading now seemed shaky, however. Did that unexpected phone call mean that what seemed Spirit-led *wasn't*? I asked Spirit. Does this news mean that I am not doing what God asks of me? "Thy will, not my will," I prayed over and over. And waited.

Meanwhile, Dr. Woodruff, Reverend Cardwell, and I began an e-mail correspondence. Let's write a book together, someone suggested. And like that messy little girl with her braids undone, the younger me who never walked if she could run, I responded with enthusiasm.

NOTES: What did I know, what did I know?

p. 20. Freedom Rides:
In 1961, the first Freedom Rider bus made a stop in Lynchburg without incident.

p. 22. *The News and Advance*:
Lynchburg's morning and evening papers, both owned by the Glass family, were bought by the Worrell chain in 1979. In 1986, *The News* and *The Daily Advance* became one newspaper. Media General bought *The News and Advance* in 1995. *Lynchburg, Virginia: The First Two Hundred Years* by James M. Elson, p. 445.

p. 26. "A leading":
A nudge, a push, an unclear impulse yet, seemingly, spiritually inspired, to pursue *something*.

✦

New World Experiences
by Phil Sosis

What lens do I need to read
the inset of your map
The one that shows the road
to Friendship, Affection, and
Touch?
Who will join me
to seek, search, look
at new spaces to explore
and new hearts to listen to?

✦

28

CHAPTER 3
"What lens do I need?"

p 26

Eight months after that tears-producing phone call with Dr. Cardwell and a series of letters and e-mails, I boarded a tiny U.S. Airways jet at Boston's Logan Airport, bound for Richmond, Virginia. "Emancipate yourself from mental slavery," Bob Marley sang over the plane's PA system as I found my seat. A message just for me? I wondered as I buckled my seatbelt. It certainly seemed so.

Finding a time for Dr. Cardwell, Dr. Woodruff, and me to meet for the first time had been looking near impossible until Dr. Cardwell, pastor of New Canaan International Church in Richmond, e-mailed that his parishioners were honoring his thirty years in the ministry with a banquet at the end of April 2001. Dr. Woodruff planned to attend, he wrote; would I like to come? Of course I said yes!

"Redemption songs," Bob Marley repeated over and over as the plane banked over Boston Harbor. With a glance at the coastline below, I pulled a crumpled sheet of blue paper from my bag. Destined to become increasingly dog-eared and tattered, that single sheet of blue paper, a double-sided workshop handout, has been my touchstone, my reality check, my magic feather a la Dumbo the flying elephant as this leading has unfolded. Entitled "White Supremacy Culture," the enormously helpful handout lists "characteristics of white supremacy culture which show up in white-led/white-owned organizations" and had been distributed at a "White Privilege" workshop sponsored by the Friends for Racial Justice committee (FORJ) at Cambridge Meeting.

Maybe this plane ride would be a good time to contemplate what, besides my party dress for the banquet tonight, I'm bringing to Richmond, I thought, rereading the handout: Perfectionism, Sense of Urgency, Defensiveness, Quantity Over Quality, Worship of the Written Word, Only One Way, Paternalism, Either/Or Thinking, Power Hoarding, Fear of

Open Conflict, Individualism/I'm the Only One, The Only Progress Is Linear, Objectivity, Right to Comfort/Safety.

Sipping my cran-apple juice, I had to admit that several attributes on that workshop sheet described me perfectly. Sense of Urgency, for example. No matter how often I reminded myself that Spirit's time was not the same as mine, and that Dr. Cardwell and Dr. Woodruff were busy people (*why* they were so busy I would come to understand only much later), the long lapses between our communications irked me. Here was a lesson I was supposed to be learning, apparently—something about patience and humility?—but filled with leading-fed zeal, it was a lesson I was not as yet ready to learn. Sometime today or tomorrow, I assured myself as the jet approached the Richmond runway, the three of us *would* find a time to set up a series of interviews.

Already, however, before I'd even met Owen Cardwell and Lynda Woodruff, this proposed book presented a major problem: me. Although it seemed that my role for this book ought to be as a dispassionate, off-stage, third-person narrator, I was already feeling little nudges that a defensive, sense-of-urgency, worshipper of the written word, i.e. Patricia Wild, once known as Pepper, was a part of the story. Again and again, when I read books on racism and White privilege, I found calls for White people to be telling *their* stories.

For example, in her Author's Notes for *Fire in a Canebrake: The Last Mass Lynching in America*, Laura Wexler wrote:

> The only way for blacks and whites to live together peacefully in America in the twenty-first century is if we begin struggling to understand and acknowledge the extent to which racism has destroyed—and continues to destroy—our ability to tell a common truth.

Or as psychologist Beverly Daniel Tatum points out in *"Why Are All the Black Kids Sitting Together in the Cafeteria?"*:

> When the dominant identity of Whiteness goes unexamined, racial privilege also goes unacknowledged. Instead, the achievements that unearned privilege

make more attainable are seen as just reward for one's own efforts.

Despite these nudges that my story should become part of this proposed book, I felt enormous discomfort at such an idea. That clueless teenager who'd stood in her high school cafeteria, paralyzed, so long ago, was now elbowing herself into a book about Owen Cardwell and Lynda Woodruff? What ego! Were shameless hubris and a decidedly unattractive need to thrust myself into the limelight the *real* reasons I thought I should insert myself into this book? How appalling! What happened to my leading to tell African Americans' stories? Others who have followed a leading, however, have told of their resistance to what seemed to be asked of them: "You want me to do *what?*" Prayer and discernment were clearly needed.

With my banquet ticket had come a handwritten note that a Deacon Sharon Boswell would be meeting me at the airport. It seemed improbable to me that on the afternoon of such an important event, a member of Pastor Cardwell's congregation would have time to come get me; I fully expected to take a cab to the Wingate Inn. But when I entered the Richmond airport terminal, there stood a tall, slender, attractive woman in sweats, her short hair swathed in a colorful scarf and holding a sheet of paper at its corners as if she were letting it drip dry. "Patricia Wile—with that last name crossed out—WILD" the paper announced. "That would be me," I said, walking up to her. Sharon reached out to hug me.

"Pastor Cardwell told us about this book," she told me as we walked towards the baggage claim. "What's it going to be about?"

"I don't know," I replied truthfully. "I'm just going to try to be open to whatever it is I'm supposed to be doing here." Sharon grinned at me; she understood. I was reminded of a passage in Elaine Pagels' *The Gnostic Gospels*: "Like Baptists, Quakers, and many others, the gnostic is convinced that whoever receives the spirit communicates directly with the divine." I may be the only White person at this banquet tonight,

I thought, but from a theological point of view, I'm a distant cousin to these Baptists.

Waiting at the baggage claim, sharing with me how God worked in her life, Sharon suddenly interrupted herself.

"I'm sorry," she interjected. "Here I am, going on and on about all this stuff. I should have asked you this before: Are you a Christian?"

Not fifteen minutes in Virginia, I thought, and I'm already being asked a variation of the Lynchburg getting-to-know you query: "What church do you go to?" Sharon's question—which I had never been asked before and therefore never really considered—was ten times harder to answer.

It's either yes or no, I thought, a little panicked. Are you or aren't you? Rapidly rummaging through my mental religious-belief file, I remembered the "Meeting Jesus Again for the First Time" workshop I'd once attended and how deeply moved I had been by "the historical Jesus." Surely my admiration, my *love* for that "teacher of wisdom" and "social prophet" elucidated at the workshop allowed an affirmative answer to Sharon's question.

"Yes," I told this Baptist deacon I'd met minutes before. "I'm a Christian."

We got in Sharon's gleaming car, the radio, I noted as we pulled away from the curb, on an all-gospel station. Sharon was eager to talk about "Pastor" and how much he meant to her, to her husband Jason and her daughter Sharice.

Having made arrangements for when she and Jason would pick me up for the banquet, the charismatic and compelling Deacon Boswell left. New Canaan did the right thing to appoint Sharon Boswell a deacon, I decided.

After ironing my dress, I decided to take a walk. For although the Wingate Inn seemed to be located in the midst of a sprawling industrial park and the view outside my window was hardly pastoral, it was a beautiful spring day in Virginia. Nostalgic for those luscious, soft breezes I remembered in Lynchburg, I decided to ignore the factories, gas stations and parking lots around me.

Cars whizzed past me as I, heading for some trees just ahead, walked along the edge of a well-paved street beside a factory's parking lot. Nervous to walk in an area where drivers were clearly not expecting pedestrians, I began to walk on the grass. The sun shone, it was warm—much warmer than Boston. This is lovely, I decided, just as I stepped into a hole and fell to the ground.

I could feel right away that I'd done more than simply twist my ankle (X-rays the next week showed a chipped malleolus) but, stubbornly, chose to believe that my throbbing, swollen ankle was a minor annoyance. "Walk it off, walk it off," I instructed myself. Limping and in pain, I returned to the motel lobby to see three African Americans sitting and talking together, and to hear one say my name. As I approached this group, a grizzle-haired man seated in an armchair extended his hand up to me: "Hi," he said. "I'm Owen."

I was shocked. I'd anticipated a thin man, a darker-skinned man, a man who would call himself "Doctor" or "Pastor." I did not expect that Reverend Owen C. Cardwell, Jr., about to be feted by his congregation, would show up at the Wingate Inn that afternoon. Nevertheless, here he was, laughing and talking with his friends while his two grandchildren chased each other around the lobby!

Reverend Cardwell introduced me to his friends. An attractive woman about my age and dressed in a well-tailored suit, Jennifer Spivey had been a parishioner when "Pastor" had preached at Concord Church in Roxbury, Massachusetts. The other friend, a slender, older man in a dark suit was Dr. Virgil Wood.

In a phone conversation earlier in April, Reverend Cardwell had announced with obvious excitement that Dr. Wood planned to attend the banquet. Virgil Wood, preacher at Lynchburg's Diamond Hill Baptist Church in the late fifties and early sixties and a close associate of Martin Luther King, Jr., had been one of the city's foremost civil rights leaders. Some might argue that Dr. Wood had been *the* civil rights leader in Lynchburg. In his book, Darrell Laurant had this to say about Virgil Wood:

> By the mid-60s, *The News* and *The Daily Advance* had begun inserting parenthetical comments into stories

about visiting speakers and local civil rights activities, consistently referring to Rev. Virgil Wood as a "local Negro agitator" and to William Kunstler [the attorney who had defended a Lynchburg African American accused of rape in 1963] as "a known associate of Communist front organizations." (p. 191)

✦

"I just want you to know," I said that evening, getting into Sharon and Jason's car, "that I am not wearing the shoes I'd been planning to wear tonight."

Jason, a handsome man, built on the tall and slender lines I'd been expecting of Pastor Cardwell, carefully drove down the Wingate Inn driveway. "Well," he replied, "I am certainly glad we got that cleared up." He and Sharon looked wonderful, he in a tux—and, as I later saw, a pair of black, white and gray-striped slip-on shoes—she in a pale yellow evening gown, its bodice revealing a butterfly tattoo on her left breast.

As we cruised down the highway, I told this handsome couple about my ankle. My new, beautiful shoes were just too painful to wear, I explained.

"Praise God that you had another pair," said Jason. Sharon concurred.

Jason's comment reminded me of a theme in gospel music which makes me cry every time I hear it: thanking God or praising God for events I would just deem lucky, circumstances I take for granted. "He woke you up this morning!" Boston's own gospel group, the Silver Leaf Singers, sing.

God is a very real presence for Jason and Sharon, I realized. If I am truly going to follow this leading, I thought, I need to pay better attention to how Spirit is working in *my* life. Perhaps a way to begin this spiritual practice would be to praise, thank Spirit more often. After all, "The Doxology," that well-known Protestant hymn, begins: "Praise God from whom all blessings flow." *All* blessings, I thought, both large or small, significant or day-to-day. Like having a back-up pair of shoes. Praise Spirit!

Just then, Sharon remembered that she and Jason were supposed to pick up a Bishop Kee so we made a hasty trip back to the Wingate. Sharon moved to the back seat while Jason went inside the motel to fetch Bishop Kee. Sitting knee to knee, she and I had one of those conversations women enjoy having with one another: about hair, clothes, nails, where we like to shop. (Both of us had bought our banquet dresses at consignment shops.) Just as it happens when my sister or my friends and I get together, neither Sharon nor I took the content of our chat, although enjoyable, all that seriously. Frivolous as our chat had been, however, every word, every phrase, every giggle was of enormous import. That girl-talk with Sharon was the first time I had ever had such a conversation with an African American woman.

Our chat ended when Bishop Alfred Kee, a dapper, elderly Lynchburg pastor, got in the front seat. He'd forgotten to pack cuff links, he told us; not only that, he wasn't feeling well. He'd made the big mistake the other day of telling "this old, blind lady" in his congregation that in former times, preachers would sometimes receive produce from their parishioners' gardens, special treats from their kitchens. "So she gave me some of her pickles," he said. "And they didn't agree with me." We stopped at a shopping mall to buy the bishop some cuff links. On our way again, Jason remarked that "they" weren't building such shopping complexes in his and Sharon's neighborhood. "We've got money," he declared indignantly. Feeling like a "they," I slumped down in my seat.

It is almost impossible to keep track of your surroundings when you're in the back seat of a car and entirely focused on what the other three occupants of that car are saying. Sharon, Bishop Kee, and Jason's conversation, like everything else I experienced that weekend, seemed significant, dramatically back-lit. Piercingly aware of how little time I'd spent with African Americans, my zeal to note and to notice was further heightened by my intention to be open to whatever I was supposed to be doing in Richmond that April weekend. This openness meant a moment-by-moment assessment: That Sharon's car radio had been set to a gospel-music station.

Bishop Kee's pickles story. What was I was supposed to learn from observations and stories such as these?

Focused on my companions' chitchat, nevertheless, when we entered an older Richmond neighborhood, I ignored my fellow passengers and looked out the window to see a long line of African American men and women snake its way into a brightly-lit liquor store. Dilapidated homes sat next to well-kept ones; the neighborhood appeared quite old and probably of historical interest. I remembered a Richmond-related story I'd read in Leon F. Litwack's *Been in the Storm So Long: The Aftermath of Slavery*. Soon after Confederate troops abandoned Richmond and Jefferson Davis had fled the Confederate capital, Black soldiers liberated Lumpkin's Jail, owned by slave-dealer Robert Lumpkin, and set its imprisoned slaves free. The two-story brick jail with bars on its windows was "located in the heart of Richmond's famous slave market—an area known to local blacks as 'the Devil's Half Acre.' " Could we be in that historic neighborhood?

We entered Cedar Street Baptist Church, chosen as the site for Dr. Cardwell's banquet so that his parishioners could celebrate their pastor's anniversary without clearing tables or serving food. Sharon's daughter Sharice, a self-assured, poised, sixteen-year-old and as attractive as her mother, greeted us at the door. Behind her, a roomful of people were singing and clapping their hands, accompanied by an organ. "You're the last ones here," Sharice shouted over the din as she escorted Jason, Sharon, and me to a table near the dais; Bishop Kee joined the other distinguished guests on the raised platform. Taking my seat, I studied this crowd of sequined, spangled, sparkly women with high, sweeping hairdos and flashing jewelry. Which one was Dr. Lynda Woodruff?

Owen, now in a tux, sat at the center of the dais. Beside him sat an elegantly dressed and coifed woman in a powder-blue evening gown worthy of a heroine in a fairy tale. Pastor and Elder Flora Cardwell looked out at the fifty or sixty people gathered there: *their* congregation. For I sensed, just by the way the couple sat together, that unlike the White Southern Baptists' recent decrees regarding the subservient role of women, Owen and Flora Cardwell functioned as equals and as a team.

In appearance, the couple presented quite a contrast. Owen is a bear of a man, rumpled-looking, even in a tux, soft-spoken, with plenty of gray in his modified Afro. Flora is trim, wears her jet-black hair in a pert flip over her forehead; her response to whatever's being said is constant, forceful, and invigorating: "C'mon, now!" "Say it!"

Dinner was served. Those delicious after-church dinners at the Hotel Virginian a faint memory, I'd forgotten about southern food. I'd forgotten the southern customs of serving iced tea—strong, heavily sweetened "sweet tea"—at dinner and of cooking vegetables longer than I've become used to. "The chicken came right off the bone," my tablemates kept commenting. After tasty fruit pie and more iced tea, the evening's program began.

There was a heated sermon by Dr. Neil Siler, a good friend of Reverend and Elder Cardwell. Virgil Wood recalled the early days of desegregation in Lynchburg and told the pastor's congregation how a very young Owen Cardwell had bravely responded to the call for social justice. There were testimonials from grateful parishioners. Many echoed my own amazement that this busy man had come to the motel earlier that day: "Pastor Cardwell came to my gymnastics meet," said Sharice. "I think that's pretty good for a pastor to do that." "He visited my son in the hospital; he prayed with him." "He visited my son in jail," an older woman commented. "And he hardly knew us!" Sister Johnsie Jones, one of the organizers of the event, read a proclamation from the mayor of Richmond that April 28, 2001, was "Dr. Owen C. Cardwell, Jr., Day."

"Does this mean I don't have to go to work on Monday?" Jason joked.

Owen stood to speak: "Whenever I don't know what to say," he said quietly, "I just sing." And he began, not a rousing, hand-clapping, Praise God! kind of a song, but the gentle, pensive: "If they wrote the story of my life." The organist picked up in the right key, others in the room joined him, and I was moved to tears. For here was a man who, at age fourteen, had walked into an all-White high school with a thirteen-year-old girl for his only visible support. Here was a man who served as a bus monitor during the hate-filled, violent Boston Busing Crisis. As an African American male, Owen Cardwell experiences discrimination and heartache on a daily basis. Yet there he stood in front of his adoring congregation singing a song which credited Jesus for his life's many blessings. The song over, Owen was reflecting on his blessed life when he looked towards the door: "Well, look who's here! Dr. Lynda Woodruff!"

A handsome woman in a gold suit who carried herself with great pride and dignity strode up to the dais, kissed Owen and Flora, then apologized to the gathering for being so late. Clearly at ease in front of an audience, her voice husky and well-modulated, Dr. Woodruff regaled the crowd with stories of Owen as a little boy: How he tried to drown her in a Lynchburg public swimming pool, how from the fourth grade on she'd known he'd become a preacher, and how, originally, forty Black students had applied to enter E. C. Glass High School but on the actual first day, January 29, 1962, it had been Owen Cardwell and Lynda Woodruff who were to show up at the high school's door.

"And Owen, always a gentleman," she said in her husky, animated voice, "let me go first!" Owen rolled his eyes; I got the feeling that Lynda Woodruff, like most gifted storytellers, leaves a story better than she finds it.

After the banquet, I introduced myself to Dr. Woodruff. That morning she'd been in the Washington, D.C. area, she explained, and had gotten lost several times driving to Richmond. Having missed the banquet, she and her friend, Violet Banks—Ms. Banks and David Young had desegregated Lynchburg's Holy Cross High School—were hungry and planned to go out for dinner. We could talk, she promised, when she and VeeVee returned to the motel.

My ankle and skinned knee throbbing, I hobbled to Jason and Sharon's car. Bishop Kee again completed our group. He seemed very tired; those pickles were bothering him again. Sharon and Jason insisted on driving me to their house, a neat, brick ranch house with a big yard and in a pleasant residential area, to get me a bottle of Advil. When Bishop Kee commented on what a nice house it was, Sharon responded, "The Lord's been good to us. A couple of months before we bought this house, we were late on our rent payment!"

Back at the Wingate, I changed into comfortable clothes, filled a plastic bag with ice, then went downstairs to wait for Lynda. I elevated my ankle, iced it, and began making notes. Instead of Lynda, however, Owen entered the motel lobby. Moments later, Bishop Kee, who said he couldn't sleep, appeared. "I have something for you," I remembered and fetched a Silver Leaf CD from my motel room, my anniversary gift for Pastor Cardwell, which I'd purchased from one of the gospel group's singers, Randy Green, the week before. Owen seemed pleased; Randy Green had been a deacon in Owen's Concord Church in Roxbury years ago.

"We didn't get along," Owen recalled, then speculated about Mr. Green's age.

"My wife will enjoy this CD," he said. Flora had grown up in Boston's Jamaica Plain.

Our desultory conversation continued: How Owen's church obtained its present building. Lynchburg's Jerry Falwell. Teletubbies. Clearly proud, Pastor Cardwell described his church's latest project: One Church - Ten Families. This pilot project enlists members of the New Canaan International congregation to mentor juvenile offenders. Owen talked about his own mentor, Virgil Wood. He mentioned Dr. Wood's expression "The Jail Trail;" I had no idea what he meant. (A subsequent trip would illuminate these words.)

Just then, a group of African American young people sauntered into the lobby. Suddenly wary, Bishop Kee and Owen Cardwell stopped talking to watch this hip-hop-clothed group, carrying a foot-high stack of videos as they paraded past us. "Now, that's just sad," commented Bishop Kee. Owen agreed.

I was taken aback; I had not expected Bishop Kee and Pastor Cardwell to denigrate members of their own race. Later, when I examined this reaction, I realized that at that point in my life, I regarded all African Americans as one seamless, monolithic, *loyal* group. After all, didn't they share the same oppression?

Very tired, the three of us said good night, confirming the time for the Sunday morning service before we parted. I left word at the Inn's front desk that I'd gone to bed, then limped to the elevator. Lynda called a short time later. She and I agreed to meet at breakfast.

After a poor night's sleep, I dressed, packed, then went to the Inn's lobby to eat the gratis breakfast. To most people, I thought, tearing open an oatmeal packet and pouring hot water into a Styrofoam bowl, this is what "Quaker" means: a picture of an apple-cheeked man in a funny hat on an instant oatmeal packet.

Lynda, dressed in another elegant suit, joined me for breakfast. Munching on a waffle, she, like Owen the night before, wanted to tell me about herself: "I hate structure," she explained. "This goes back to my days at Glass. I hate being told what to do. But I can do it. Certainly when I got my Ph.D. I had to."

Pulling my date book out of my bag, I asked her how and when the three of us could set up a time to meet.

"That's not possible," she replied. Her appointment book remained in her office at North Georgia College and State University; it weighed seven pounds. "It never leaves my office," Dr. Woodruff stated flatly.

Did I take a moment to imagine a seven-pound appointment book? Did I try to understand *why* this handsome woman was so incredibly busy? Did I wonder what kinds of experiences Lynda Woodruff might have had in the past with writers and journalists? Did I acknowledge that both of us were nervous during this first meeting, understandably wary of one another? Did I praise Spirit that Lynda Woodruff and I were having breakfast together and that in a few minutes, she and I would be going to church together. *Owen's* church? No. I was completely caught up in my own Sense of Urgency, too focused on this book project and my own agenda to appreciate the preciousness of that Sunday morning. Instead of celebrating this first meeting, I was disappointed and, to be honest, a little irritated that an interview date hadn't been set.

[A few years later, Lynda would read an earlier draft I had written which described our initial meeting in Richmond; she was justifiably horrified—and hurt—by how I'd portrayed her. "Intimidating," I'd called her, for example. And given how little I understood of her life, why, she wondered, had I'd presumed to write what I'd written? Why had I been so judgmental? So critical? Why, indeed.]

It was a bright Sunday morning but to my surprise when I stepped outside to get into Jason's car, decidedly chilly. Bishop Kee, still feeling under the weather, again sat in the front seat. He commented on his declining health as we drove to church. "I used to be an ant on a hot stove," he said. "Now I have to slow down." I laughed in appreciation.

On our way to church, Bishop Kee and Jason swapped truck-driving stories; Jason drove a truck for a living as had Bishop Kee as a younger man. Listening to these two men trade tales of icy roads and tight, difficult turns, I acknowledged a simple fact: many African American churches, like Bishop Kee's, cannot adequately support their preachers. Black clergy like Bishop Kee are often forced to find supplementary work.

This realization begged me to look at Friends Meeting at Cambridge: I could afford to fly to Richmond that weekend, for example, because my mostly White, mostly affluent faith community had given me the money to do so. Had I acknowledged that privilege? No. Rather, I'd prided myself that Friends Meeting had "awarded" me a grant without giving particular thought as to why such funding should even be available.

Again I was more focused on the conversations around me than what could be seen from Jason's car window. But I saw that New Canaan International Church was located in a very pretty, tree-lined, residential area with houses on quarter-acre lots. We pulled into the trim, brick church's parking lot; Sharon was waiting for us, a mink stole draped over her shoulders.

New Canaan International's walls are a gleaming white. It has orange and white stained-glass windows and large, white acoustic tiles on its ceiling. Its benches are varnished wood. Bishop Kee disappeared to another part of the church, I took a seat near the front with Lynda and her friend, Violet; Elder Flora Cardwell, in a black-trimmed red suit, sat behind us. Having celebrated so heartily the night before, many parishioners apparently decided to sleep in that morning.

"Where is New Canaan?" asked Owen, looking out at the sparsely-filled church.

Virgil Wood's sermon touched on Lot, demons and pigs, Humpty Dumpty, Nixon's allowing the Mafia to sell drugs in the inner city, "our little babies in jail," and "black men like spiders caught in a web," and again, "The Jail Trail." Listening to Dr. Wood's impassioned sermon that morning, I began to understand why the Lynchburg civil rights leader had been such an important person in Owen and Lynda's lives. For here was a man of passion and erudition, someone as likely to quote *The New York Times* as the Old Testament, someone imbued with the spirit of *his* mentor, Martin Luther King, Jr.

Bishop Kee underscored Dr. Wood's fiery message: "I've got grandsons in jail," he said mournfully. Owen commented that Lynchburg had just built a multi-million dollar jail. Bishop Kee, sensing a kind of a lull, got things moving again by leading us in a Praise God, hand-clapping song.

[After reading the earlier draft, Lynda reminded me that during the service, she and I passed notes to each other, a school-girl silliness she had relished and which I had not remembered. This omission indicates how very differently she and I recalled that Sunday morning: Lynda had felt that we were beginning to get to know each other, I was nursing my annoyance that her seven-pound appointment book sat in Dahlonega, Georgia.]

New Canaan's organist and drummer had to leave to play at another church so a young boy from the congregation sat down at the drum set and began to play as the adults of his faith community stood and, pew by pew, placed money in the donation plates. I joined the crowd. When it was Pastor Cardwell's turn to speak, his demeanor, unlike Dr. Wood and Dr. Siler from the night before, was calm, pensive, casual.

After he'd finished speaking, Owen invited me to speak to his congregation. I rose, my heart pounding, to explain that my Quaker meeting had given me the money so that I might make this trip. Patterning the length of my remarks on what I might say if moved to speak at a meeting for worship, I spoke briefly, then sat down. I sensed, however, that I'd left most of Owen's parishioners confused: Quaker? Meeting? Where, exactly was Cambridge? And why would a bunch of White people from this unknown place send this woman here anyway? Longing to jump up, to say more, to make myself more clear, I also knew that, on a weekend when New Canaan was honoring its pastor, what I might add to my original remarks was of no importance. So I remained seated.

Lynda and Violet had to return the car they'd borrowed so they left right after the service. As we said goodbye in New Canaan's parking lot, I tried to swallow my disappointment that Lynda and I had spent so little time together. After lunch with several members of New Canaan's congregation, Sharon Boswell drove me to the airport; the New Canaan deacon and I parted with genuine regret.

The walk from Sharon's car through the terminal's long corridors and up the small jet's stairs was too strenuous for my chipped ankle. It throbbed by the time I finally sank into my seat. Fastening my seat belt, I reflected on the blessedly few times in my life when pain or illness seemed to separate me from the rest of the world. While recovering from gall bladder surgery, for example, I had watched healthy people carelessly, easefully going about their business, taking their pain-free existence for granted. How irritating, how shallow, how clueless those healthy people had appeared!

Perhaps this pain is actually a gift, I thought, as the jet taxied towards the runway. I am now obliged to look at the events of this staggering weekend from the perspective of someone not-quite-me, someone who takes nothing for granted, someone deeper, less blasé.

It was a glorious day to fly, the East Coast shoreline clearly delineated below, the Atlantic sparkling in the sunlight. This leading, a journey towards Something, had begun.

NOTES: "What lens do I need?"

p. 29. My "Magic Feather" Handout

"White Supremacy Culture," adapted from a compilation by Tema Okun and originally written for *changework*, 1705 Wallace Street, Durham, NC 27707

pp. 30. 31. *"Why Are All the Black Kids Sitting Together in the Cafeteria?"*

Given my own cafeteria story, Dr. Tatum's book demanded that I read it.

p. 31. *The Gnostic Gospels* by Elaine Pagels, Vintage Books, NY, 1981, p. 23

p. 32. "Meeting Jesus Again for the First Time" was a 3-day workshop conducted by Tom Ewell in 1996 and based on the book by Marcus J. Borg with the same title. Its subtitle*: The Historical Jesus and the Heart of Contemporary Faith.* (Harper San Francisco, 1994) This invaluable book, along with Tom's workshop, allowed me to embrace a particular version of Christianity I find compelling and sustaining.

p. 34. "The Doxology"

In most Protestant churches, the words to "Old One-Hundredth" are:

> *Praise God from Whom all blessings flow.*
> *Praise God all creatures here below.*
> *Praise Him, above ye Heavenly Hosts.*
> *Praise Father, Son, and Holy Ghost.*

The Unitarian hymn I grew up with was very different:

> *From all that dwell below the skies,*
> *Let faith and hope and love arise.*
> *Let beauty, truth, and good be sung,*
> *Through every land, by every tongue.*

"Why do they always have to change the words," my mother, who was raised Congregationalist, complained every Sunday.

My father, whose family had been Unitarians for generations, merely shrugged.

p. 36. Lumpkin's Jail

Been in the Storm So Long: the Aftermath of Slavery by Leon F. Litwack, Vintage Books, NY, 1980, p. 168

pp. 36, 37.
"SOUTHERN BAPTISTS TRUMPET A VICTORY DECLARING WIVES MUST 'SUBMIT,' GROUP CAPS CONSERVATIVE TAKEOVER" June 14, 1998, *Boston Globe*
...Last week, the convention sent shock waves across the country when it voted to amend its essential statement of beliefs to include a proclamation that a woman should "submit herself graciously" to her husband's leadership and that a husband should "provide for, protect and lead his family."
...The declaration is the culmination of the takeover of the Southern Baptist Convention by fundamentalists who believe the Bible must be taken literally as the inerrant word of God.

✦

From Bloodbirth
by Audre Lorde

That which is inside me
screaming
beating about for exit or entry
names the wind
wanting wind's power
wanting wind's voice
it is not my heart
and I am trying to speak
without art or embellishment
with bits of me flying out in all directions
screams   memories   old pieces of pain
struck off like dry bark
from a felled tree   bearing
up or out holding or bringing forth
child or demon

✦

Reprinted by permission.

CHAPTER 4
"Old Pieces of Pain"

In her "biomythography," *Zami: A New Spelling of My Name*, Audre Lorde tells how, in the early fifties, she first learned of Crispus Attucks:

> "The first cat to die in the Revolutionary War, in Concord, Massachusetts," explains her friend, Ginger. "A Black man, name of Crispus Attucks. The shot heard 'round the world. Everybody knows that."

Lorde is mortified. And angry:

> I had spent four years at Hunter High School, supposedly the best public high school in New York City, with the most academically advanced and intellectually accurate education available, for "preparing young women for college and career." I had been taught by some of the most highly considered historians in the country. Yet, I had never once heard the name mentioned of the first man to fall in the american [sic] revolution, nor ever been told that he was a Negro. What did that mean about the history I had learned?

What, indeed. A decade after Ginger's brief—and somewhat inaccurate—history lesson, while sitting in the back of a Whites-in-front-Blacks-to-the-rear Lynchburg Transit bus, I received a similar history lesson from a student at Lynchburg's *other* high school. No seats available in the front, I'd sat down beside a Dunbar High girl about my same age. (At sixteen, did I think that sitting beside an African American on a segregated bus would somehow promote racial harmony? Sadly, I think I probably did.) On her lap was a pile of books and resting on top of that impressive stack, a clipboard with mimeographed pages attached. The young woman, who'd deemed it wise to pretend we weren't sitting shoulder-to-shoulder, was no doubt irritated as I craned my neck to read the top, purple-inked sheet on her clipboard, the story of Crispus Attucks, shot in *Boston*, not Concord, by British soldiers. For Lorde, a woman of color, her friend Ginger's story of a Black Revolutionary War figure engendered anger. How come I was never taught this? For me, that mimeographed sheet on a clipboard produced similar indignation and, in a moment of grace, a flash of insight. A zealous and no doubt young African American teacher at Dunbar High School, frustrated by the American History books on hand, dog-eared discards from E. C. Glass, produced his or her own materials, running them off on the school's mimeograph machine. When the young woman sitting next to me had first received the account of Crispus Attucks, she'd held the sheet of paper to her face to smell the heady, intoxicating aroma of mimeo ink; students did that in those days. And then she, like Audre Lorde, like me, learned something left out of her battered history text.

On *my* lap that day rested a pristine, shiny, newly-issued American History textbook. A junior at E. C. Glass at the time, I was required to take American and Virginia History; our teacher was "Miz" Wallace, a formidable, tightly-corseted southerner with gray hair arranged in prim sausage curls rolled away from her plump face. The following year, Miss Wallace—who, Lynda remembers, displayed a Confederate flag on her sunny classroom's wall—would become Lynda and Owen's homeroom teacher.

Printed on a piece of tawny oaktag thumbtacked just below Miss Wallace's clock were the words "Still waters run deep." After one year at E. C. Glass, I understood enough of my new high school's culture to know that such classroom postings meant "Abandon hope for lively discussion in *this* class." Thirty or so of us sat in rows, I remember, facing Miss Wallace's desk, the classroom's windows to our left. Every day, Miss Wallace grilled us on our homework. She'd start with the first person in the row closest to the windows and, working from front to back, proceed up each row. If you knew the answer—"What year did the Pilgrims land?"—you got a 100, if you didn't, you got a 0. I remember the unnerving pause between each question as Miss Wallace, who never budged from her desk, carefully recorded that day's grade. Often these questions were based on a mimeographed list of historical events and their respective dates: "1610: 'Starving Time,' Jamestown settlement." "1619: First slaves arrive in Jamestown," which we dutifully memorized. Miss Wallace said nothing about slavery. She did note, however, that since the White Jamestown settlers had arrived several years before the Pilgrims—"1620: Pilgrims land at Plymouth Rock"—and were, she assured us, every bit as religious, just as grateful as those northern Pilgrims, there had undoubtedly been a *Virginia* Thanksgiving first. And she glared in my direction: a warning to the class's Yankee not to argue.

What history had my shiny American History textbook left out? What historical facts had been omitted from Miss Wallace's mimeographed sheets? What other stories and historical events had that nameless, inspired Dunbar High School teacher chosen to mimeograph? When they had crossed that E. C. Glass threshold in 1962, what stories, what history did Owen Cardwell and Lynda Woodruff carry with them? What had been their historical context? I didn't know. Like most White Americans, I spent most of my life not knowing. So I decided to do my homework for this leading.

Not surprisingly, as a typical Worshipper of the Written Word, I began my exploration in libraries, both in greater-Boston and in Lynchburg, where I found countless books on racism, Virginia history, and the civil rights movement. Early in this self-study, when the fact that Lynchburg had been founded by a Quaker family seemed notable (a fact I later realized to be but a minor footnote), I also studied up on Quakers in Virginia. Because "Lynchburg recommends itself for study for a variety of reasons. The most pragmatic is that the town has retained a wealth of private and public records," meant I could access helpful books on the southern city from the Somerville Public Library just blocks from my house. To supplement what I was learning from books, I spent hours at Lynchburg's Jones Memorial Library scanning microfilms of the two Lynchburg newspapers from the fifties and sixties.

One day while looking at a microfilmed page from *The Lynchburg News*, I realized I needed to cross-reference something so I opened Darrell Laurant's *A City Unto Itself: Lynchburg, Virginia in the 20th Century.* A quotation in Darrell's book about Lynchburg's newspapers, spoken by an unnamed African American city councilman, caught my eye: " 'A white woman, any white woman, was referred to [in Lynchburg's newspapers] as a Mrs. or Miss. No black woman was ever anything but plain Ann Smith.' "

Looking again at the microfilmed newspaper accounts I'd *just* been reading, I realized, to my shame, that this nameless Lynchburg councilman's observation was accurate. Lynda Woodruff was consistently referred to as "the Woodruff girl" or "Lynda." The society page account of my sixteenth-birthday tea dance at Boonsboro Country Club, however, referred to me as "Miss Wild." And I hadn't even noticed. Not for the first nor the last time during the leading, I'd failed to "stay awake."

Humbled by that experience, I began to better understand how accurately the Worshipper of the Written Word label applies to me. As in the case of the Lynchburg paper's "the Woodruff girl," for example, unless I pay vigorous attention, I willingly accept what I see as written and am often blind to subtleties and nuances of racist language and usage. Since that experience in the Jones Library, I am grateful when I come upon written words like Audre Lorde's "american revolution." Without prodding, it is still a struggle to stay awake, to notice, to pay attention to how written words are actually *written*!

Further, when I began to examine this written-word-worship label more closely, I realized that to a distressing degree, I ascribe legitimacy, primacy, authenticity to the printed word, particularly if that printed word is found on pages which have been collated and bound and sandwiched between sturdy pieces of cardboard and catalogued by the Library of Congress. Indeed, from the very beginning, this leading, vague and uncertain in so many respects, had been clear about one thing: Whatever else might happen, one outcome for this leading would be a collated, bound, catalogued book!

But it was *unbound* manuscripts not catalogued by the Library of Congress and not unlike those purpled mimeograph sheets used at Dunbar High School long ago which proved particularly revealing and insightful while I did my homework for this leading. Three of the most helpful manuscripts had been written by African Americans; two shared the same title: "No Matter How Long." One paper, "Against All Odds: The Success Story of Dunbar High School" by Delano Douglas, was among the papers, tapes, and other jewels I discovered at Lynchburg's Legacy Museum of African American History. Another unbound manuscript, "Blacks in Lynchburg, Virginia, 1933 – 1945," a thesis by Dr. Leslie Camm, noted Lynchburg historian, was hand delivered by its gracious author one morning as I investigated the Legacy Museum's treasures.

Housed in a carefully restored, gingerbread-rich Victorian, the Legacy Museum, which opened in 2000, offers a changing array of poignant and illuminating exhibits; on its second floor, a treasure-trove of materials and documents on Lynchburg's African American history are archived. At first glance, to discover the museum's unbound papers seemed a happily-ever-after ending to my mimeographed-sheets-on-a-clipboard story.

But was it? It's heartening, of course, that two score years after my history lesson on the back of a segregated bus, a small city like Lynchburg now claims this jewel of a museum, the first such exhibit hall and archives in central Virginia. Nevertheless, to see the piles of papers, manuscripts, and tapes on the Legacy's shelves made me wonder: Whose stories end up on a museum's shelves and whose stories end up on a library's shelves?

Just behind the Legacy Museum lies Lynchburg's Old City Cemetery. Historically significant to both the city's White and Black citizens, the meticulously restored cemetery, its artfully landscaped grounds worthy of Frederick Law Olmsted, offers one of the loveliest sites in Lynchburg in which to contemplate whose stories are told. And in what format.

Built on the hills and hollows typical of Lynchburg, also known as Hill City, the cemetery contains the graves of both noted and long-forgotten Lynchburg citizens, three-quarters of them African American, and relics from the city's past: Here is a column from the Paul Laurence Dunbar High

School, razed in 1979. There is the extravagant tomb of Agnes (1789-1874) and Lizzie Langley (1833-1891), mother and daughter "madams" in one of Lynchburg's famous "sporting houses." An old railroad station near the cemetery's Lotus Pond and Butterfly Garden is an heirloom from before the Civil War, a reminder of the time when heavily industrialized Lynchburg with its many tobacco-processing factories had been a prosperous, bustling transportation center. The cemetery's antique railroad station house symbolizes how critical transportation has always been to Lynchburg: First the James River and Kanawha Canal, dug by slaves, and then, later, three railroad lines and several turnpikes linked the central-Virginia city and its factories with the greater world. For runaway slaves, Lynchburg was another kind of transportation center. The city's proximity to the Blue Ridge Mountains meant an escape route to Ohio and Pennsylvania and freedom via secret trails and caves.

While following this leading, I traveled to Lynchburg five times. On each visit, I made a point to visit the Old City Cemetery, to swing on a long-roped swing suspended from a tall pecan tree, and, surrounded by the graves of Lynchburg citizens, Black and White, to ponder the latest history lessons this leading illuminated.

On one trip, on a steamy summer day, I visited Harlem Renaissance poet Anne Spencer's charming garden not far from the little house where she wrote. Although I had once lived a few miles from her home on Pierce Street, I had never heard of the Lynchburg poet, passionate gardener, and friend of Langston Hughes and James Weldon Johnson.

I understood, of course, that in the years I'd lived in segregated Lynchburg, our paths would have been prohibited from crossing. And I understood that even *had* Lynchburg not been a segregated community at that time, the elderly Anne Spencer might not have chosen to spend time with an adolescent Yankee transplant who liked to write. Still, sitting in her lovely garden, I cried as I contemplated how racism, this "hidden wound," diminishes my life.

When doing my homework for this leading, what I was learning often made me angry. Like Audre Lorde, furious when she discovered how limited her supposedly excellent education had been, I'd become incensed "about the history I had learned" or *hadn't* been taught. Other accounts, other history lessons were simply heartbreaking: narratives related by slaves who had lived in Lynchburg and told in *Negro in Virginia*, or a description of the dangerous working conditions for Lynchburg's tobacco-processing hands, to name but two. But like that moment in Anne Spencer's garden, there were times when the depth of my ignorance made me weep. Often, like that moment, I was discovering something about *Lynchburg's* history, something I'd been denied learning, something that had happened just a few miles from where I had once lived or gone to school.

NOTES: Old Pieces of Pain

p. 49. "Lynchburg recommends itself..."
Stephen Tripp, *Yankee Town, Southern City: Race and Class Relations in Civil War Lynchburg*, p. 4

p. 50. "Unnamed African American city councilman"
I have since wondered if this city councilman might have been Edward Barksdale, Lynda Woodruff's stepfather.

p. 50. "Staying awake," i.e. being ever-mindful of racism
Polly Atwood, unpublished qualifying paper, Harvard Graduate School of Education, "Journeys We Make Daily: Five White Women's Narratives as Resources for Anti-Racist Teachers," May 2003, p. 90.

p. 50-51. Unbound manuscripts:
One "No Matter How Long" is by Owen's father, Owen C. (O. C.) Cardwell, Sr. This manuscript tells the story of Lynchburg's civil rights movement through a series of transcribed interviews with many of the city's most notable African Americans. The other "No Matter How Long: The Struggle to Integrate the Public Schools in Lynchburg, Virginia, 1954–1970" was Lynchburg native Henry Heil's master's thesis. Another thesis, "Blacks in Lynchburg, Virginia, 1933 – 1945," by Dr. Leslie Camm, relates the history of

Lynchburg's African American churches, stories from Dunbar High School's earliest days, and how the Depression devastated Lynchburg's African American community. The unbound and enormously helpful paper, "Against All Odds: The Success Story of Dunbar High School," had been written by Delano Douglas when a student at Lynchburg College, and found on the Legacy Museum shelves.

p. 52. Anne Spencer died in 1975 at the age of ninety-three.

p. 52. "Hidden wound"
From the book of the same title by Wendell Berry.

NOTE: Much of what I learned re Lynchburg's civil rights history can be found at www.tiljusticerolls.com

✦

1975
by Anne Spencer

Turn an earth clod
Peel a shaley rock
In fondness molest a curly worm
Whose familiar is everywhere
Kneel
And the curly worm sentient now
Will light the word that tells the poet what a poem is

✦

CHAPTER 5
"Light the word," light the way

May 2001:

It's the spring semester of my daughter Allison's senior year of high school. For the past few months, her responses to my "Good Morning!" or "How was your day?" have been brusque, monosyllabic, and often delivered over her shoulder as she rushes to her next meeting or runs to her room to check her e-mail. Tonight, however, my usually distant daughter stands beside my desk as I write about my trip to Richmond, her fists clenched, and talks:

"This is big, Mom. Even the kids who aren't into anything want to do this. I've been going to that school for four years now, and all that time, have been mostly separated from the Black kids. We want to talk about this! There's so much—"

Remembering another phone call she needs to make, Allison rushes off again. My seventeen-year-old daughter, with other students from her public high school, is organizing a forum on race.

Allison is a senior at Cambridge Rindge and Latin High School in Cambridge, Massachusetts, that hip city on the Charles River known as "The People's Republic of Cambridge," the home to Harvard University and MIT and Friends Meeting at Cambridge, lofty bastion of the politically correct.

But, as Allison and her classmates note at their race forum, even in a public school system as progressive as Cambridge's, in 2001, integration is still only an aspiration. Almost fifty years after *Brown versus Board of Education*, as one student observes of Rindge, "There's two separate worlds." Indeed, the Linda Brown of *Brown* fame, in 1994, mused: "Sometimes I wonder if we really did the children and the nation a favor by taking this case to the Supreme Court. I know it was the right thing for my father and others to do then. But after nearly forty years we find the Court's ruling unfulfilled."

"You can't put your finger on it," comments another Rindge High forum participant, talking about race, "but it's huge."

"It's an honor to talk about something people don't much want to talk about," Dianne Wilkerson, an African American and a Massachusetts state senator tells the race-forum students. "We need public dialogue. We have to have conversations."

A proud mother of one of the organizers, I sit in the high school's cafeteria and listen to the race forum speakers. In front of me sits an African American student wearing a black tee shirt with the words "By Any Means Necessary" printed in white letters on the back.

During one forum speech something compels me to lean forward and tap this young man on the shoulder: "Excuse me, but do you know about Malcolm X?"

It is a stunningly stupid question, it is a stunningly inappropriate impulse and I knew this before I leaned forward. Yet I am moved to ask anyway.

The young man turns around; incredulous, he stares at me for a few moments. "Yeah," he snorts, then turns away.

Cheeks burning with embarrassment, I resume listening, unaware that, in fact, my asinine question lights the way to where my leading will take me.

✦

For Quaker abolitionist John Woolman, one of his leadings began with enviable clarity and according to his journal, with actual light. While staying at a fellow Friend's house in Burlington, New Jersey, in 1757, Woolman was awakened one night by a "clear easy brightness." A voice spoke to his "inward ear" promising him "Certain Evidence of Divine Truth." Thus urged by both a light of "about nine inches diameter" and "the language of the Holy One spoken in my mind," John Woolman traveled to Virginia to meet and to pray with slave-owning Quakers.

Shortly after this night-time vision, John Woolman sought and received a "certificate," i.e., a letter of introduction, from the members of his Mount Holly, New Jersey, meeting, thus testing his leading to travel south with his own faith community. This certificate not only explained Woolman's intentions and concerns, it also served as a notice to the Mount Holly community that, once again, its visionary but peripatetic member would be absent from his wife and seven-year-old daughter for several months; please remember the Woolman family in your prayers.

It was customary in the eighteenth century for traveling Quakers to be the guests of other Quakers without charge. Deeply uncomfortable to stay in Friends' homes where slaves were owned, Woolman "spoke to one of the heads of the family privately and desired them to accept of them pieces of silver and give them to such of their Negroes as they believed would make best use of them; and at other times I gave them to the Negroes myself, as the way looked clearest to me."

Perhaps during the process of obtaining his certificate, Woolman and other members of his meeting had "seen clear" that the best way to address Woolman's "deep and painful exercise" was to give this money although "a trial both to me and [these slaveowners]." Perhaps his supply of a "large number of small pieces" had even been supplied by his meeting. Certainly, by sitting with others in prayer, John Woolman's eventual journey to Virginia—where he *may* have stayed with the Lynch family matriarch, Sarah Lynch—was held in the Light by the Mount Holly meeting.

Very new to the idea of a Spirit-led process, the first time I tested my leading with my faith community was to ask for money! Created in 1998 by an anonymous donor, my meeting's Special Sources Fund awards grants "to support individual projects within the Meeting community." The April 2001 trip to Richmond had been paid for by this grant.

My application to the Special Source Fund, submitted in the fall of 2000, documents how I perceived this leading *before* I had met Lynda and Owen:

Remembering the Society of Friends' role in the abolition and civil rights movements, what is our present-day role? Are we needed? If so, where? It is my hope that *Lest We Forget* [the proposed book's title at that time] might shed some light on these questions. And as a member of Friends Meeting at Cambridge, I would seek ways to share what I have learned in the process of writing this book with my meeting.

Like so many uncomfortable moments as this leading unfolded—listening to the tapes of my first interview with Lynda and Owen, for example, which makes excruciatingly plain how little I understood their anguish at E. C. Glass High School—I cringe, now, when I realize what my grant application reveals about my beliefs, assumptions; my cluelessness. Although faint, mere whispers of what I was thinking, where I was at that time, imbedded in my seemingly innocuous application are so many unacknowledged tenets, so many beliefs I had not yet examined.

One such whisper: That as a Friend, I had somehow magically inherited John Woolman's Light-filled spirit, Quaker abolitionist Lucretia Mott's stirring witness, or civil rights worker—and convinced Friend—Albert Bigelow's courage. In other words, since I, too, worshipped in silence for an hour on Sunday mornings, I was automatically enlightened concerning racism and White privilege!

Another whisper: Although I had carefully followed Quaker form by posing a question: "What is our role? Are we needed?" I was really saying: "We of the largely White, affluent, well-educated Friends Meeting at Cambridge community *are* needed." Wasn't I repeating the paternalism of many White activists?

Like a gentle Virginia breeze, Spirit moves through faith communities; it whispers the same message to more than one Inward Ear. At the same time I began my spiritual journey, several people in my meeting had already begun to explore the charged subjects of racism and White privilege. At the urging of the newly formed Friends for Racial Justice (FORJ) committee, my spiritual community (which happens to be located in one of Cambridge's most exclusive neighborhoods) began enormously clarifying conversations about race, about class, about privilege, about being White. Painful, humbling, awkward, revealing, maddening, transcendent, and all the feelings in between, these conversations began to open my eyes and my heart.

To be honest, I was initially reluctant to attend a FORJ meeting. Talking about race with a bunch of Quakers at first seemed pretentious, silly, weirdly detached from reality. But as I quickly discovered, I had much to learn from other White people about my own cluelessness. I discovered, for example, that I was not the only Quaker who believed that I'd automatically inherited the Society of Friends' civil rights mantle.

It was at a FORJ workshop where I picked up the "White Supremacy Culture" handout. As mentioned before, since the earliest days of this leading, I carried that blue-colored handout wherever I went, like Dumbo's "magic feather."

✦

The second time I tested my leading with members of my faith community was in the summer of 2001 when I met all-too-briefly with my "Dream Team," five extraordinary people from FMC who had agreed to serve on a clearness committee for me. And why had these people been asked to meet? Again, it was because of a grant application! One of the stipulations for a Lyman Grant, a Quaker-sponsored fund which supported leadings, was that as part of the grant-application process, applicants form a clearness committee. Dutifully I made some phone calls.

"I'm sure you would have asked for a clearness committee even if you hadn't been going after this grant," one Dream team member said. Sadly, he gave me more credit than I deserved.

Still shaky about where this leading was headed, one thing I *could* tell my Dream Team: I had already bought my plane ticket for my second trip south, this time to Lynchburg.

Soon after I had returned from Richmond, Deacon Sharon Boswell had casually mentioned during a phone call that her beloved "Pastor" planned to preach in Jerry Falwell's church in July. Jerry Falwell? "Old-Time Gospel Hour" Jerry Falwell?

Moral Majority's Jerry Falwell? The Jerry Falwell who, in 1965, questioned "the sincerity and nonviolent intentions" of civil rights leaders such as Dr. Martin Luther King, Jr. and James Farmer? *That* Jerry Falwell?

I had to be there.

NOTES: "Light the word," light the way.

p. 57. My daughters' father also lives in Cambridge; Allison and her twin sister Christina were therefore entitled to attend what was considered a superior public high school.

p. 57. "Two separate worlds"

It is my understanding that since my daughters graduated, CRLS has taken active and positive steps to address this separateness.

p. 57. Brown *versus Board of Education: A Civil Rights Milestone and Its Troubled Legacy* by James T. Patterson, Oxford University Press, NY, 2001, p. 207.

pp. 58, 59. from *The Journal and Major Essays of John Woolman,* edited by Phillips P. Moulton, Friends United Press, Richmond, Indiana, 1989, pp. 58, 60, 61.

p. 59. Woolman was not *completely* insensitive as to how his leadings and, therefore, his absences affected his wife and child. When, in 1763, Woolman informed his wife Sarah that he felt led to travel into Indian territory, "she appeared to be deeply concerned about it, but in a few hours time my mind became settled in a belief that it was my duty to proceed on my journey, and she bore it with a good deal of resignation."! (p. 124) In 1769, although moved to go to the West Indies, Woolman stayed home because "the time of leaving my family hath not yet appeared clear to me." (153n)

p. 59. "14th day, 5th month. Was at Camp Creek Monthly Meeting and then rode to the mountains up James River and had a meeting at a Friend's house, in both which I felt sorrow of heart, and my tears were poured out before the Lord, who pleased to afford a degree of strength by which way opened to clear my mind amongst Friends in those places." (p. 63)

At the time of Woolman's journey to Virginia, Sarah Lynch, mother of Lynchburg founder John Lynch, was a wealthy widow living across the James River from the present day Lynchburg, in the foothills of the Blue Ridge Mountains. Later that same year, Sarah Lynch gave land to the Lynchburg Quakers to build a meeting house. Despite her generosity, however, Sarah Lynch was later disowned by her meeting when she married a non-Quaker.

p. 60. Albert Bigelow had been riding on the 1961 Freedom Ride bus when it stopped, without incident, in Lynchburg.

p. 61. Clearness committee: A collective-discernment process as a small group decides if it is "clear" that a proposed action—a couple wishing to get married, for example—is actually a good idea.

p. 61. My "Dream Team":
    Sylvia De Murias, an artist I greatly admire for her clarity, the writer Martha Mangelsdorf, well-grounded in Quaker theology, Kitty Rush, central to our Meeting's Peace and Social Concerns committee's work at that time, the photographer Skip Schiel, who documents social injustice whether in Palestine or on Cambridge Common, and Jonathan Vogel-Borne, whose prophetic voice so often speaks to my condition.

◆

*Isaiah 61:1 — The Spirit of the Lord God has taken control of me!
The Lord has chosen and sent me to tell the oppressed the good
news, to heal the brokenhearted, and to announce freedom
for prisoners and captives.*

◆

CHAPTER 6
Good news?

The Restoration Jubilee: Setting the Captives Free conference was over. Owen Cardwell, who'd spent months organizing the two-day conference, sat in the study of his mother's Lynchburg home sipping a cooled fruit drink. Clearly worn out, Dr. Cardwell was nevertheless pleased: "To say I am happy would be an understatement," he declared.

"I have always responded to human need and stuff just started happening." He smiled, adding, "I don't think any of us set out to make history." By "us" he meant the five organizers for the Restoration Jubilee Conference. Cardwell, Dr. Virgil A. Wood, Bishop Alfred Kee, and Dr. James E. Coleman, Jr., are African American evangelical preachers. The fifth was Dr. Jerry Falwell.

"Jerry's concerned about his legacy," Owen Cardwell observed that hot day in July of 2001. "I believe that is genuine."

What had moved Jerry Falwell to lend his name to this conference? With capital-letter emphasis, a Restoration Jubilee conference press release proclaimed:

OUR GOAL IS TO ESTABLISH A DYNAMIC AND WORKING COALITION FOR THE SUCCESSFUL RE-ENTRY OF INMATES BACK INTO THEIR COMMUNITIES, AS WELL AS PREVENTION OF THE JAIL TRAIL ON THE FRONT END, AND IN THE PROCESS, JUMP-STARTING THE LOCAL COMMUNITY'S ECONOMY.

The press release continued:

Dr. Wood and Dr. Falwell both say, 'we [sic] may have been on opposite sides of the movement back in the Civil Rights days but God has put us both on the same side of Restoration Jubilee now.'

A racially mixed crowd of sixty or so street workers, recently released convicts, prison preachers, representatives from prisoner-rights agencies from all over Virginia, plus a handful of Lynchburg citizens, Black and White, attended the conference. Most of that crowd already understood the situation; for me, the figures quoted during the two days were shocking: 1.3 *million* people were currently incarcerated in this country; 600,000 prisoners would be released in 2001. Most distressing is that 70 percent of those released prisoners would find themselves going through a revolving door—right back into jail. Seventy percent! As one former inmate, once again behind bars, wondered aloud in a video shown at the conference: "How did I get here, again?"

"This is not a Black issue, it's not a White issue. It's a problem for all of us," Owen Cardwell observed, glancing at his mother's study walls covered with plaques and framed mementos attesting to the Cardwell family's contributions to Lynchburg's civil rights movement, including several pictures of him and Lynda Woodruff.

Reverend Cardwell's pastoral identity began in 1968, on Senior Day at E. C. Glass. A tradition at the Lynchburg high school unchanged by desegregation, soon-to-be graduates wore costumes, attended a special assembly; there was surreptitious drinking, even a parade downtown.

"I dressed up as a country preacher...This guy was dressed up as the Devil and I was a country preacher and we hung out all day. Together. That was really the best day that I had at Glass. Because it was also about this time I finally made Honor Roll. I finally made Honor Roll," he recalled.

Owen's White classmates probably didn't know that country preachers—also known as exhorters—had been a fixture in Virginia's African American community since antebellum times. Requiring no training other than "the call to preach," itinerant preachers traveled the Virginia circuit, "preachin' black men into their graves." These African American laymen exhorted at the graveside of slaves who had died since their last visit, the palm of their hand outstretched to symbolize "God's book."

After Nat Turner's insurrection in 1831, Virginia's Governor Floyd told the state legislature: "The public good required that the Negro preacher be silenced, because, full of ignorance, he is incapable of inculcating anything but notions of the wildest superstition." Virginia's African American preachers were banned soon thereafter.

However, as ex-slave West Turner noted in *The Negro in Virginia*: "Dey law us out of church but dey couldn't law 'way Christ." Slaves "stole away" at night to "Hush Harbors," i.e., prayer meetings in the woods. Country preachers were now "stump preachers." The remains of a chopped-down tree served not only as a readily available pulpit for an itinerant preacher but also as a form of protection from Virginia's "patterollers," patrolmen on horseback who enforced the state's slave code. "They [worshipping slaves] would run around or jump over the stumps, an' if the patterollers come in they were likely to break their horses' legs," explained another ex-slave.

"There are really two kinds of people in the world," Cardwell reflected as he sat back in his chair. "There are those who observe history and those who make it."

✦

Psalm 121:1 — I look to the hills!
Where will I find help?

The Restoration Jubilee Conference began at Lynchburg's biggest and best-known Baptist Church: Jerry Falwell's Thomas Road Baptist Church (TRBC), the former site of the Donald Duck Bottling Company. The TRBC complex dominates the summit of one of the city's rolling hills and overlooks the blue-collar Fort Hill neighborhood, not far from the restored Quaker meeting house on Fort Avenue. TRBC's redbrick Pate Chapel—where Owen Cardwell preached—shares the hilltop with the vast 12,000-seat TRBC Sanctuary, a cinderblock TRBC bookstore and welcoming center, and a shopping mall-sized parking lot.

For its evening session, the conference moved downtown to Court Street Baptist Church, built on a steep hill rising from the James River. Court Street is considered the "Mother church" for all of Lynchburg's African American congregations. The church's centrality to the city's African American community meant that its pastor at the time of the conference, Dr. James E. Coleman, Jr., *had* to be included in the preparations for the Restoration Jubilee conference. "Dr. Coleman was probably in diapers when the rest of us were starting out," Owen Cardwell joked in his mother's study.

"We are the light from a city on the hill," Virgil Wood exhorted during the conference. "We are part of what God is already doing. This is a movement from the heart of God."

✦

Matthew 11:2 — John was in prison when he heard what Christ was doing. So John sent some of his followers to ask Jesus, "Are you the one we should be looking for? Or must we wait for someone else?"

"There are three men who have had a profound influence on my life," says Owen. "My father, Bishop Alfred Kee, and Virgil Wood." Wood, beloved civil rights leader and pastor at Lynchburg's Diamond Hill Baptist Church, now preaches at Pond Street Baptist Church in Providence, Rhode Island. "Dr. Virgil Wood has always encouraged me," says Dr. Cardwell.

Virgil Wood is equally clear—and grateful—about his own antecedents. He often tells the story, when as a young man, he met a former slave. "I knew I was listening to history," he says of their conversations, his voice tremulous as he recalls those talks. During his Jubilee address, Dr. Wood slowly read off the names of eighteen Lynchburg civil rights activists now deceased: "Owen C. Cardwell, Sr. ...Fred Harris, the bail bondsman...R. Walter Johnson, Sr. ..." When he completed the list, Dr. Wood concluded: "We stand on their shoulders."

But for Dr. Wood there is one now-deceased civil rights activist, not from Lynchburg, who stood head and shoulders above them all: Martin Luther King, Jr. During his Jubilee Message address at Court Street, Virgil Wood presented a copy of a photograph of himself and Dr. King—taken at a civil rights demonstration—to Jerry Falwell. "To my Friend and Co-Worker Virgil Wood In appreciation for your significant ministry and your unswerving devotion to the ideals of freedom and justice," is hand-written on the back of the photograph and signed, simply, "Martin."

Since leaving Lynchburg, Dr. Wood, whose doctorate is from Harvard, has lent his talents, energy, and wisdom to a variety of causes: He's annotated the Jubilee Bible; "This is what kept African Americans from ending up on reservations like the American Indian," he says, holding the leather-bound tome. He's preached. He's taught. And, increasingly, he's become involved with the criminal justice system; recidivism. He's traveled around the country, he's met former inmates and social workers. It was Virgil Wood who coined the phrase "The Jail Trail," by which he means the path of poverty, inadequate education, and systemic racism which leads to eventual incarceration. It was Virgil Wood who introduced Judith Sedgeman to the conference (more about her work later). Virgil Wood brought the "Glidepath to Recovery" video to the conference, which featured Father Peter Young's work with returning prisoners in Albany, New York.

Despite his years as "an earth-shaker," Virgil Wood remains spry and vibrant although now in his seventies. Spreading the word about The Jail Trail clearly energizes him.

"This [conference] is the answer to a prayer," said Dr. Virgil Wood. "Let me heal the soul of our nation."

✦

Leviticus 25:39 — Suppose some of your people become so poor that they have to sell themselves and become your slaves. Then you must treat them as servants, rather than slaves. And in the Year of Celebration [Jubilee] they are to be set free, so they and their children may return home to their families and property. I brought them out of Egypt to be my servants, not to be sold as slaves. So obey me and don't be cruel to the poor.

The interior of TRBC's Pate Chapel is shiny and white, its apple-green carpet spotless. Glowing, rectangular panes of tan, green, blue, and purple glass with Christian symbols—a cross, praying hands, etc.—cover the chapel's windows, plastic ivy and calla lily plants have been placed on either side of its podium. Bishop Alfred Kee stood at the podium, the last speaker before the conference dinner break.

Prior to Bishop Kee, conference attendees had been welcomed by Jerry Falwell. They'd heard Owen Cardwell preach on Mark 10:46, the story of the blind beggar, Bartimaeus—" 'Shut up, blind man! Stay in your place!' "—and learned of Reverend Alfred Terrell's work with at-risk youth and juvenile offenders in Newport News, Virginia:

"Our church says [to men and women recently released from prison] 'We got job skills for ya, we got a job for ya, we got a GED for ya, we got love for ya,' " the Newport News preacher elucidated.

An ex-offender had addressed the gathering: "What I've heard is powerful and poignant," she said, tears in her eyes. "It can happen. When I got out, I needed my pastor and my community resources."

Now it was Bishop Kee's turn.

You might call Bishop Kee a sort of *jazz* evangelical preacher. For while the Fellowship Church of Christ pastor is as well-versed in the Bible as his colleagues and he dresses much like his fellow pastors dress in dazzling white shirts and dark, pinstriped suits, Alfred Kee stands apart from the rest with his particular gift for being able to really stay in the moment, to sense what's not being said, and to weave those unspoken thoughts and ideas into his remarks. Which is why, no doubt, Bishop Kee was asked to be spiritual advisor to the Restoration Jubilee Conference. And why he is such a significant person in Owen Cardwell's life and *his* spiritual advisor.

A grandfather with three of his grandsons in federal prison, Bishop Kee looked at the conference attendees:

"What is restoration, anyway?" he asked. Then he stopped, considered: "My son told me not to sing this song," he said. "I'm gonna sing it anyhow." The Lynchburg pastor stomped his foot a couple of times and then he began:

"I went to the enemy's camp and I took back [Stomp] what he stole from me," Owen's spiritual advisor sang. "Took back [Stomp] what he stole from me. Took back [Stomp] what he stole from me."

By the time Bishop Kee repeated the first line of the minor-key song, everyone, Black and White, sang along with him. I joined in, too. Bishop Kee's song seemed to mean: We're in Jerry Falwell's tent right now, a man who once tried to steal Black people's dignity. And this is the moment when that history, that theft, must be acknowledged.

✦

Acts 9:3—When Saul had almost reached Damascus,
a bright light from heaven suddenly flashed around him.

Jerry Falwell wears beautifully tailored suits, his eyes are amused, his skin pocked; he has a full head of gray hair. When the Old Time Gospel Hour preacher speaks, one reason for his immense popularity becomes evident: Jerry Falwell has a fabulous voice. It's deep, resonant, soothing. Reassuring. His voice says: I *know.* I have it all worked out.

He's smooth: "What is your name?" he asked me as he greeted the first arrivals to Pate Chapel Thursday afternoon. "I should have known that," he responded mournfully when I supplied my name, firmly shaking my hand. The world-famous pastor then quickly moved on to the next group of people. Jerry Falwell's ability to glad-hand strangers comes from long practice: As he noted in his address to the conference Thursday evening, it was his willingness to go door-to-door in the earliest days of Thomas Road Baptist Church—"a hundred doors a day, six days a week"—that brought in the worshippers. It was this one-to-one contact that people in need remembered.

"Somebody in the family dies, they say, 'Now what was the name of that preacher, again?' and they go looking for my card in a drawer somewhere."

Court Street's sanctuary is painted white, its glossiness muted by the church's amber-colored stained glass windows. And by time. Sitting in the spacious sanctuary as it slowly filled, I counted off the years that have passed since 1880 when African American craftsmen built the church: How many prayer meetings, how many speeches, how many community gatherings, how many civil-rights ventures had this "Mother church" witnessed before tonight? Had I ever set foot in a place of such historic import to African Americans? Had I ever breathed in the atmosphere of such a sanctified space? No.

The last time Jerry Falwell spoke at Court Street Baptist Church was in 1986 when he and the Reverend Jesse Jackson took turns addressing a gathering of the Virginia N.A.A.C.P. "Now, he can preach when he wants to preach," Dr. Falwell recalled of his co-preacher that night "fifteen, sixteen years ago. When he's not messing around he can really preach. He can."

Dr. Falwell continued: "That night, I told the story of my pilgrimage from typical southern segregationist to where I am today. It is a journey, you know. And I was born and raised here. In the sixty-eight years, I have a good memory of where we were. And where we've come from. Now, we'd all like to forget it. But I recall—I recall when eating in a drugstore, riding on a bus, visiting a church or whatever the case might have been would have been a challenge for African Americans in this town and just about every southern town...Thank God that's a long-ago memory.

"One of the reasons for that is Dr. Virgil Wood. He's done some teaching at Harvard. When he mentioned the other day up there that he was working with Dr. Jerry Falwell on a project, they stopped him and said, 'Say that again'...

"Obviously we have a major problem [concerning recidivism.]...It's not a Black problem or a White problem, it's not a skin problem, it's a sin problem. And it's universal.

"Amazing, then, that the church has not, long ago, realized what the problem is, diagnosed it, and provided a solution. It's not all that easy. But it's doable," concluded Reverend Falwell.

"He's got inroads to senators," said Bishop Kee of his conference colleague. "Somebody's got to be on the inside. Whether you like him or not."

✦

John 13:34 — But I am giving you a new command.
You must love each other, just as I have loved you.

Despite its historic nature, there was a tentative quality to the conference. Both Dr. Wood and Dr. Cardwell made it clear that the two days were merely the first, baby steps of a long journey. As Dr. Cardwell explained: "We're not trying to present a plan, we are presenting a Man."

"God is in the delivery business," Owen had declared in his Restoration Message on Thursday afternoon. He did not say *service* delivery business. For although there was some talk of 501(c)3s among church leaders, some discussion of "best practices," actually spelling out *how* "the church will come out of the walls" was left a little vague. Apparently implementation, or as Donald Bush, chairman of the Virginia Coalition for Juvenile Justice put it, "the diffusion of innovation" is the next step on this journey.

In his remarks, the affable, flaxen-haired Donald Bush, who is also Owen's friend, gave a particularly Virginian flavor to this next, as-yet-unclear-step. Bush, a Scottish Presbyterian Theologian, anticipated a possible roadblock on this Restoration journey: resistance by local officials. " 'Who's your daddy?' " a skeptical politician might ask. " 'Do I know your mama?' "

73

Sitting in his mother's study, Owen Cardwell remembered: "I was a part of the traditional, mainstream church for twenty-four years. And I didn't like what we were doing. We were too far from the New Testament. Too into ecclesiology. Raising money. Worrying about who's in charge. I just got tired of it." Cardwell's dissatisfaction led him, six years ago, to found the New Canaan International Church in Richmond.

His prison ministry began modestly. A couple of years before the conference, members of the New Canaan congregation had volunteered to provide Christmas gifts for families where a caretaker had been incarcerated. "It was nice," he says. "But no follow-up." When Owen began preaching at a nearby juvenile facility, he discovered what Jerry Falwell and John Woolman knew: the power of one-to-one contact. "I developed relationships with those kids." At about this same time, Reverend Alfred Terrell, a former classmate of Dr. Cardwell at Boston University, had begun *his* prison ministry in Newport News. "Next thing I knew," Owen grins, "we [New Canaan] were starting One Church - Ten Families." New Canaan's effort was one of five demonstration projects in the country, each one unique. One Church - Ten Families, funded by the Children's Defense Fund, is another best practice in Dr. Cardwell's opinion. Its design is simple and straightforward: Trained mentors, selected from the New Canaan congregation, work with recently released juvenile offenders—and their families.

"We're not beating anyone over the head with a Bible," Reverend Terrell assured the conference. But, of course, the whole idea of churches getting involved with this country's court system, its schools, and its social services worries the people who think the separation of church and state is becoming increasingly blurred. Indeed, the same week the Restoration Jubilee Conference was being held, the U.S. House of Representatives, while discussing President Bush's Faith-Based Initiative, began debate on the hiring practices of churches and houses of worship. Of particular concern were the homophobic beliefs of certain fundamentalist sects. Large questions remain unanswered: What about a formerly incarcerated person who's an atheist? Gay? Or a Muslim? Or

Jewish? A feminist who considers God-as-Father, God-as-Lord sexist, demeaning language?

"The best Bible they [ex-offenders] can read is me," counters Reverend Terrell. "Jesus formed a relationship with folks."

"It's time to retool the churches to do what churches were supposed to be doing all along," urges Owen Cardwell.

◆

John 1:5—The light keeps shining in the dark,
and darkness has never put it out.

Conference attendees were offered best practices. And a best practice accompanied by a Big Idea: "The twelve-step program keeps you in the past," Dr. Wood commented during his Court Street presentation. "Not healing." But, he promised, attendees would hear something new the next day, a Big Idea, a metaphor about possibility, about hope, about innate health very different from what Alcoholics Anonymous says about recovery. "How to take the mess from around the soul," he hinted from the historic church's pulpit, then launched into a spirited account of a fifty-cent piece lying in the gutter for many years. "It may appear tarnished, worn, and dirty," Wood told his listeners, "but underneath all its grime and filth it's still a fifty-cent piece."

After Father Young's video had been shown the next morning, Judith A. Sedgeman, Director of the Sydney Banks Institute for Innate Health of West Virginia University, talked more about that fifty-cent piece. A handsome, middle-aged White woman with short, blonde hair, she spoke with conviction and humility: "We come into life with a pure consciousness," she said. "But we make bad choices. We feel bad about ourselves."

In the Innate Center's work with prisoners at the Santa Clara prison in California, she said, "We are redefining health. We touch the health in people."

She told the story of "a defining moment" in her own life, a time when she touched the health in a troubled young man. Late one night, walking home from her college-aged daughter's apartment near New York's Washington Square Park in Greenwich Village, Judith knew she was being followed. She turned around to see a young man, his hooded sweatshirt pulled over much of his face, close behind her. She invited him to walk with her and engaged him in conversation. When she discovered he lived in a cardboard box in Washington Square Park, "I gave him all my money; he was going to get it, anyhow." The young man escorted Judith safely to the door of her hotel, promising to look into getting his GED.

She addressed the conference: "You are one thought away from your pure heart. Like that fifty-cent piece Dr. Wood talked about last night."

"Her words are different, but the language is the same," Owen Cardwell commented in his mother's study.

For me, Judith A. Sedgeman spoke the language of George Fox:

> This I saw in the pure openings of the Light without the help of any man, neither did I then know where to find it in the Scriptures; though afterwards, searching the Scriptures, I found it. For I saw that Light and Spirit which before Scripture was given forth, and which led the holy men of God to give them forth, that all must come to that Spirit, if they would know God, or Christ, or the Scriptures aright, which they that gave them forth were led and taught by.

For me, Judith Sedgeman was saying what I heard time and again at Cambridge Meeting: "Walk cheerfully over the earth, answering that of God in everyone."

✦

Joshua 6:1—Meanwhile, the people of Jericho had been locking the gates in their town wall because they were afraid of the Israelites. No one could go out or come in.

If Bishop Kee is a Louis Armstrong or a Miles Davis, James Coleman is jazz drummer Art Blakey. Throughout the conference, Dr. James Coleman, Jr. kept the beat, graciously taking charge of the conference paperwork, registration details, who'd ordered a box lunch. For the conference's final event, Dr. Coleman led conference attendees, two by two, from his Court Street church to Lynchburg's new Adult Detention Center just a couple of blocks away. Reporters and cameramen from the local media walking alongside, we walked past regal, antebellum houses—many of them now law offices—on uneven, irregular slate sidewalks. Jerry Falwell, I noticed, was not among us.

Since my broken ankle the year before, uneven surfaces had become challenging. Walking cautiously, I fell into step with someone I would have preferred not to walk beside. The day before, this pinstriped, bow-tied man, a member of a prominent Lynchburg "03" family, had suggested that "chronic anger and depression have a molecular basis" and that the resultant biological change in a chronically angry, depressed person could be measured. "Basically, their 'Fright or Flight' mechanism has been burned out," this conference participant claimed. Why, he wondered, weren't we using medicine to address this problem?

As Zora Neale Hurston often noted: "My race but not my taste." Sitting in the Pate Chapel, I cringed at the wrongheadedness of the 03-er's remarks. Isn't this White man simply blaming the victim, I wondered. And why isn't he, why aren't I, why aren't all of us who are the beneficiaries of a system which produces such "chronic anger and depression" for Others squarely addressing such oppression?

Owen, chronically unflappable and soft-spoken, said, "I have a concern that African American kids are over-medicated as it is. But," he added gently, "it's important to dialogue, however."

Now, walking beside the nattily-dressed man, I introduced myself. By way of explanation as to why I was there, I mentioned that I had graduated from E. C. Glass the same year Owen had desegregated the all-White high school.

"I think your sister was in my class," I added. The 03-er verified this. And then his eyes widened: "Do you mean that my sister was actually in school during an historic time?"

My anger towards him from the day before softened, although in that moment I could not have explained why. Now I wonder if by looking into his widened eyes I saw him step back from his scientific certainties and measurable outcomes to briefly contemplate that the dark-skinned man who had oh-so-gently put him down the day before had a *story*. Owen Cardwell—who very well might be chronically angry and depressed—was a "Negro desegregator." In that eye-widening moment, did this bow-tied man connect the dots of Jim Crow, *Brown*, Owen, Owen's life experience leading to the conference or, conversely, Jim Crow, *Brown*, some other Black man, the Jail Trail?

Now, with some pain, I also see that this 03-er's access to Owen's narrative was through two White women, his sister and me. His little sister had been there; he had a connection to January 29, 1962. And I, by virtue of attending a conference Owen had helped to organize, credentialed Owen, I'm afraid, in his eyes.

He and I and the rest of the conference conferees arrived at our destination. Scrawny trees, badly in need of watering and care, had been planted around the brand-new jail. Although several official-looking cars were parked outside and in a parking lot across the street, there was little sign of activity. Like the rest of downtown Lynchburg, the Detention Center block was eerily bereft of people.

Staring at the Detention Center's redbrick walls, a vivid childhood memory came to me. When my family had lived in Stow, Massachusetts, we often drove past the gray, gloomy, walled, turreted, barbed-wire prison in Concord. "There are *people* behind those walls," I'd acknowledged with that piercing and deep understanding special to children.

"There are *people* behind those walls," I now acknowledged.

Cameras clicking and whirring, the Restoration Jubilee conference attendees stood outside those bricked-up walls. At the entrance to the center, Elder Flora Cardwell—herself an ordained minister—prayed. Dr. Coleman prayed. The group of thirty-five to forty people then moved to the Detention Center's side entrance to sign the "historic New Jubilee Covenant" which concluded: "We can make a difference, as one human being 'yoked' to another, by our common destiny, as direct descendants of One God of Love. So Help Us God —AMEN, AMEN, AMEN!"

Amen.

✦

Isaiah 61:1 — The Spirit of the Lord God has taken control of me! The Lord has chosen and sent me to tell the oppressed the good news, to heal the brokenhearted, and to announce freedom for prisoners and captives.

Was I being asked to bring the good news of this conference back to Friends Meeting? Was I being nudged to *do something* about prison ministry? Instead of reporting to my Quaker meeting how we might be "helpful" to the African Americans in Lynchburg, had I discovered that instead, Owen Cardwell, Jerry Falwell, and their conference co-leaders could illuminate Friends Meeting at Cambridge's path?

NOTES: Good news?

p. 64. Bible passages taken from The African American Jubilee Edition: Contemporary English Version.

p. 66. "Preaching black men into their graves."
Negro in Virginia, p. 85

p. 66. Dr. Owen Cardwell's career:
The young man who performed "Tossin' and Turnin' " at the Senior Day Assembly received a BA from Virginia Seminary and College in Lynchburg, a master's degree in Theology from Boston University, a master's in Education from Cambridge College in Cambridge, MA, and an honorary doctorate in Sacred Literature from Richmond's Spirit of Truth Institute in 1997. He is currently working on his dissertation, "Maintaining Family Connectivity," at Liberty University.

p. 67. Patterollers
Negro in Virginia, p. 163

p. 67. In 2001, Thomas Road Baptist Church claimed 22,000 members.

p. 67. The TRBC complex also included a two-story brick building belonging to Falwell's Liberty University, formerly Liberty Baptist College, created in 1971. The university's main campus has now incorporated GE's plant on Candler's Mountain, site of Carter Glass's former farm. (Elson, p. 403)

p. 68. Dr. James Coleman is a close friend of Reverend Al Sharpton.

p. 68. Lynchburg civil rights activists
For more information, see www.tiljusticerolls.com

p. 69. "Earth shaker"
Bishop Kee said this.

p. 72. Falwell quote regarding Jesse Jackson:
"Why would you print this junk in a book about Lynda Darnell Woodruff?" Lynda wrote in the margin of an earlier draft. "Please don't perpetuate his crimes."

Given Owen's close relationship with Dr. Falwell, however, and what Lynda and I were to discover about Owen's and Dr. Falwell's shared beliefs, it seems important to include this quote from Lynchburg's most famous preacher, who died in May of 2007.

p. 73. "The church coming out of the walls"
Reverend Terrell said this.

p. 73. "Who's your daddy?"
Bush's African American listeners might have recalled the days when "Who's yo pappy? Who's yo pappy?" was often asked of slaves whose fathers might also have been their masters. (*The Negro in Virginia* p. 94.)

p. 76. The George Fox quote:
from *Faith and Practice of New England Yearly Meeting of Friends*, pp. 66, 67.

p. 76.
The "Walk cheerfully..." quote is also from George Fox and is inscribed on Cambridge Meeting's portico which connects our Friends Center with our meeting house. Although plainly inscribed, Fox's words are sometimes misquoted on a Sunday morning: "...listening to that of God" or "preaching to" or "seeking that of God" are among the most common mistakes. Sadly, in the many years I have attended Cambridge Meeting, I have never heard anyone comment on Fox's admonition to walk *"cheerfully."*

p. 77. "03"
Lynchburg's nicest neighborhood. My family's split-level Lynchburg home had been located in the prestigious 24503 zip code.

✦

Give over thine own willing,
Give over thine own running,
Give over thine own desiring to
know or be anything
And sink down to that seed
Which God sows in thy heart.
And let that be in thee,
And let that grow in thee,
And let that breathe in thee,
And let that act in thee.
—*Issac Penington*

✦

CHAPTER 7

Sinking Down

"School integration came quietly to snow-crusted Lynchburg today," declared *The Daily Advance* on January 29, 1962. Accompanying the afternoon newspaper's account of Lynda and Owen's first day at E. C. Glass is a photograph of thirteen-year-old Lynda Woodruff and fourteen-year-old Owen C. Cardwell, Jr. Lynda, wearing "a red carcoat," emerges from her mother and stepfather's "small blue sedan." "The Woodruff girl" stands beside the opened back-seat door; rather than face the newspaper's cameraman, she looks down at the pile of notebooks—no clipboards—she carries. Owen, "a tall, slender youth," also holding a notebook or two, stands beside the "neat, dark-eyed girl." His hair cut very short and wearing a dark jacket and neatly pressed slacks, the young Owen stares off into the distance, an apprehensive look on his face. *The Daily Advance*'s photograph of that historic event reveals the two neatly-dressed "Negro teenagers" against the stark and unexpected background of snowbanks, whitened trees, snow-covered ground, and school steps.

In that same photo, seated in the driver's seat, his face in shadow, was Edward M. Barksdale; Georgia Barksdale sat beside him. That frigid, momentous January morning in 1962, the teenaged Cardwell and Woodruff were alarmingly visible; in the shadows, however, were the Cardwells, the Barksdales, and many other parents from the African American community. "You all didn't do anything without your parents being there," Georgia Barksdale reminded her daughter forty years later.

Forty years after that historic January day, Lynda, Owen, and I sat in the family room of the Barksdales' snug ranch-style home, my tape recorder on the coffee table between us. The keynote speakers for Randolph-Macon Woman's College's Black History Celebration, the two "firsts" had arranged for me to interview them the evening before their speeches. Lynda's mother, Georgia Barksdale, after offering me a glass of cranberry juice, hovered in the adjoining kitchen. A window-sized opening between the kitchen and the family room connected the four of us.

Almost giddy to be finally sitting down with Owen and Lynda and embarrassingly ignorant of these firsts' historical context, I was too excited and too ill-prepared to really grasp much of what happened that night. Only later, for example, did I appreciate how fitting it had been that only feet away from where we sat, Lynda's mother washed dishes or offered something to drink or chimed in occasionally. Georgia Barksdale represented those other behind-the-scenes adults like Virgil Wood, the N.A.A.C.P. Legal Fund lawyers, Martin Luther King, Jr.—the grown-ups who had orchestrated Lynchburg's school desegregation process.

Something delightful and unexpected happened that evening because Georgia Barksdale was nearby: I was given the opportunity to witness Owen and Lynda in relation to someone from the older generation. No longer teenagers, of course, the two firsts were nevertheless deferential to the handsome, energetic civil rights advocate bustling in the kitchen. By observing their respectful, diffident behavior with Lynda's mother, I caught a glimpse—just a taste—of Lynda D. Woodruff and Owen C. Cardwell, Jr., at thirteen and fourteen.

No strangers to being interviewed, Lynda and Owen briskly reviewed the events leading up to January 29, 1962, beginning with the transfer requests from Cecilia Jackson, Brenda Hughes, and themselves. Owen spoke of that last vestige of Virginia's massive resistance still operational in the early sixties: the Pupil Placement Board.

"Actually, the law at the time did not require— [the Pupil Placement Board] did not have to give a reason [to reject our transfer applications]," the Richmond preacher recalled. "And that is why they systematically rejected any applications that came from Black kids."

Lynda elaborated on Lynchburg's court case. "They published our IQs, test scores, report card grades, everything in *The Lynchburg News*," she stated. "We were originally turned down because 'we weren't smart enough'...And Virgil Wood took them to task and said, 'How could you have criteria and academic standards for a public school?' So then they had to back off the IQ rejection..."

"Understand the ramifications of that," Owen noted, sorrowfully. "We had to be so much better than our White counterparts."

The rest of the evening probably should have been spent talking about those teenagers' public humiliation, their vulnerability, their early-on lesson that as firsts they were expected to be exemplary. There were so many other things that Lynda and Owen wanted to say, however, and none of us had a clear idea when the three of us would be able to meet again. So the interview continued.

"There were originally thirty-two applicants [requesting transfers from Dunbar to Glass]," Owen recalled. "And then it went down because economic pressures were applied."

"For all the parents, right," Lynda commented, "they were scared of [losing] their jobs. Naturally! In Lynchburg, Virginia, if you lost your job, where would you get another one? In 1961? 1962?"

"But they would have been able to sue, I think," argued Georgia from the kitchen.

"Nobody would have won," countered her daughter. "It would have been rattling through the courts for twenty years while everybody went bankrupt."

"That's how [Olivet] Thaxton lost his job," Owen reminded his hostess.

"The economics of it was true for all four of us," said Owen. "Dr. Jackson [Cecelia Jackson's father and a dentist], of course, was solely dependent on the Black community for his livelihood, so was my father who was assistant manager of the [Virginia Mutual Benefit Life] insurance company then."

"My dad was a federal government employee," noted Lynda. "During that era, a federal employee could have been fired for campaigning, politicizing. The rule is there. They choose not to use it until they want someone fired. Then they bring it out, dust it off... Whether we were overt or covert, there was the threat of economics for my parents."

Lynda's comment reminded me of a story I'd read in *Negro in Virginia*. In the 1890s, 150 African American mine workers lost their jobs because they'd voted contrary to the mine owner's wishes. How easy it had been to file that story under Terrible Things That Happened After the Civil War. How much more uncomfortable it was in 2002 to acknowledge what that "threat of economics" still meant to so many people of color in this country.

I was curious about what sort of preparation Owen and Lynda had been given before they'd arrived at Glass: "Did you receive any training about what would happen if people were violent?" I asked them.

"We weren't trained, we were dictated to," Lynda replied. "We were told, 'You will not respond, if the media asks you anything, it's *No comment*, or *Everything is fine*, and we did exactly that. Whenever we were asked by anybody how things went, the answer, according to Martin Luther King, was: 'Everything went well. It is *fine!*'

"That was published in the media. And twenty years later, the idiots who are now leaders, instead of asking either one of us, as if we were dead, for the truth, they read the paper and were known to take national stands, and be on television, discussing civil rights and the desegregation of the schools, and how wonderful and nonviolent it was. They didn't ask me if it was nonviolent. Excuse me!" Lynda exclaimed.

It was at this point that Georgia Barksdale made her comment regarding her parental role. "You know, you all didn't do anything without your parents being there."

"That's right," Owen chimed in.

"We were there," Mrs. Barksdale repeated, entering the family room. She stood by the coffee table and directed her next remarks to me: "You know why they were asked not to talk about it? They didn't want other children *not* to apply. Had they known that these kids were having problems—see, we used my basement. And we brought in other kids to fill out applications to keep the applications flowing. So Martin Luther King didn't want it, and the lawyer in New York—" No one could remember this lawyer's name. [It was James M. Nabrit III.]

Lynda compared the Lynchburg teenagers' training with that of John Lewis, Jesse Jackson, and other followers of Dr. King.

"But ours was not as involved," interjected Owen.

"We simply were given a prescription," Lynda agreed. "This is what you say when asked and this is what you do. And God bless everybody but everybody can claim whatever they want. Only two people walked into that hostile environment on January twenty-ninth."

Lynchburg's White establishment, the 03-ers, loathe to repeat the overt violence and the national headlines of Little Rock, orchestrated a very different scenario for *its* desegregation process. Just before Lynda and Owen were to begin classes at Glass, for example, a party in their honor was given by the city's elite. Owen and Lynda rattled off the names of the White students who'd been invited.

"But they were my classmates," I protested. "Seniors." And therefore, of course, not in any of the two new students' classes, and therefore not available for support or advice.

"They very carefully protected our classmates," observed Lynda.

"What is probably not very well known," Owen pointed out," and I don't know all of the details of it, because we weren't privileged to all of the details, but once it was determined that we were going to go to Glass, everything was pretty well coordinated. Even classes that we were going to have."

"By whom?" I asked.

"The superintendent of schools and L. H. McQue [Glass's principal]," Lynda supplied.

Forty years later, Dr. Lynda Woodruff looks back at the White establishment's arrangements with a trained eye: "The whole orchestration was programming our failure."

"That's her opinion," Owen commented.

"I am a teacher," she continued. "Let me give you my evidence. There is no reason on God's green earth why—why would you start a school year in January? When we got there, we were thirty-two chapters behind [in their Latin class]. I failed Latin flat as a fritter. It was the first time I had ever failed a class.

"Now, go back. We had started talking about Eric Erickson's Stages and Ages [before the interview]. Go back and think of a high-achieving pair. And that's why I say that."

Dr. Woodruff and Reverend Cardwell, although linked by race, were treated quite differently by their new school's administrators, particularly in the person of "Guidance Counselor" (GC).

"GC wanted me suspended the first day for the length of my skirt," remembers Lynda. "GC called me in. I wore a kilt. Remember the little kilts? With the big pin? I was called indecent, immoral, lewd and lascivious. The first day! That's what I wore. And that's what GC did."

Although it's hard to tell from the photograph taken of Lynda and Owen after their first day at Glass, it appears that Lynda's kilt was mid-knee length, shorter than most—but not all—of the skirts displayed in my 1962 yearbook. Pam Thayer, for example, a very popular senior and one of the 03-ers invited to Lynda and Owen's party, wore her skirts just as short. Did GC call Pam Thayer, daughter of a Randolph-Macon professor, "indecent, immoral, lewd, and lascivious"? I doubt it. In the early sixties, as Lynchburg's civil rights leaders probably should have warned Lynda and Owen, most Glass students, male and female, dressed conservatively. Skirt-lengths would become far more risqué, of course, as the decade progressed.

"I suspect that GC had to do within the culture what GC had to do," argued Owen. "I think that it was more GC relating to me as a male and relating to Lynda as a female than it really had to do with GC relating to us as African Americans. Or 'coloreds' at that time. Because I had opportunities to go to GC for interpersonal things that were going on with me, and GC was very supportive."

"Like what?" I asked, frankly curious but also uneasy about my question. Should I really be asking about "interpersonal things?"

Reverend Cardwell was, however, glad to respond. "Well, there was this one kid—ironically, years later, I saw this guy walking from—what was the name of that mental hospital in Madison Heights?" he asked Lynda.

"Lynchburg Training School," she answered.

"This guy was in Lynchburg Training School! But he was a guy who was in my study hall. He would ask me these stupid questions! About how much they were paying us to go to school. And I had a split study hall with lunch in-between. And so, invariably, I would come back from lunch and if I weren't paying attention, there'd be a tack on my seat. And I kind of thought that he was the one who was doing it. So I'd go to GC about that kind of thing.

"I went to GC the day John Kennedy was shot. I went to GC because I popped a guy. I was more scared that I might cause something racial than I was that I might be put out of school. This was in-between class. Somebody had shouted out, 'They killed your hero, didn't they!' And I turned around—this guy was just finishing his statement and I just popped him. And I immediately went to GC and told GC what had happened before anybody could tell on me because I was scared. I said—" Owen lowered his voice, made it raspy—" 'Yeah! What I do? I'm the only lil' Black dude, here!' " He resumed his normal voice: "And GC was very understanding.

"GC helped me make the decision to take Creative Writing. We didn't have Creative Writing at Dunbar. I took Creative Writing my senior year."

Mention of a class not offered at Dunbar recalls the original N.A.A.C.P. lawsuit against the Lynchburg Public Schools. Owen Cardwell, Jr. had stated he wanted to take Mechanical Drawing. The lawsuit reasoned that because Dunbar High did not offer this class, the young man should be allowed to transfer to Glass.

"Mary Spottswood Payne," I interrupted; I'd taken Creative Writing *my* senior year with the gifted, warm "Miz" Payne, who had treated me with kindness and respect and had encouraged me to continue writing.

"Yes!" he affirmed with warmth. "I loved her, loved her. I absolutely loved her!"

For both of us, reviled African American student and out-of-sync Yankee transplant, Mary Spottswood Payne represented those White southerners not nearly as well known as the Bubbas and the southern-fried racists. Mary Spottswood Payne could be counted among the South's decent, gentle people, people who revered knowledge and erudition, people who, in matters of race, managed to do the right thing, courageous, principled southerners like Virginia Durr, Anne Braden, Mab Segrest.

But there were teachers at E. C. Glass who were not Mary Spottswood Payne: "I did research on shoulder latent-muscle soreness from holding an arm in an unnatural position." Lynda mimed holding her arm up in the air, then directing her attention to that arm as if examining this part of her body for the first time. "Got relatively famous for it. Same thing with wrists. Class participation—"

"Didn't [teachers] call on you?" I asked.

"Never. I got Cs and Ds in courses at E. C. Glass," she went on. They stopped giving me Ds after the second year. But I got plenty of Cs that I did not earn. I can name on five fingers the teachers that evaluated me fairly...June Moon for P. E. [Physical Education]. Now she did for me what Owen was describing [re GC]. Standing there with that whistle in her mouth. And she would ask me, 'Are you okay?' She checked on me.

"The teachers wouldn't even make eye contact in the hall. The teachers! Never mind the kids calling us 'Nigger!' every day. We expected that. See, the civil rights movement told us, 'You're going to be called names, they're going to throw spit balls, they're going to do things to you.' All of it was focused on the students. We were ready for that. I could get right behind Owen! Tall? You've got the picture on the brochure right there! I had lots of protection."

She pointed to the Randolph-Macon brochure listing its Black History Month events which lay on the coffee table in front of her. On the brochure's cover was a black-and-white print of Owen and Lynda descending E. C. Glass's snowy steps after their first day, Lynda in her carcoat and "indecent" kilt. A grim smile on her face, she hugs a pile of books to her chest; the tall Owen, looking down as if deep in thought, is right behind her.

"No one prepared me for teachers. It was not in a child's paradigm that a teacher could be unfair," Lynda stated.

"That's the part of the whole child thing," Owen pointed out. "You've got to remember that here we are, going through the normal passages. But not having normative social interaction. On the one hand, I'm having White people question who I am. And on the other hand, I'm having Black kids asking 'Who do I think I am?'

"Georgia and my parents, for the most part, really helped this, because they would have parties here. Many times, we had parties down in the basement here and over at my father's house because he had put his office over there by then. And so we could go down in the office and have parties and stuff.

"They were doing educational tracking at that particular time. So we were in the A track. A lot of the kids that were in the A track with us at Dunbar, still had social interactions with us at parties and stuff here. And at my mother's house."

"Right, right," added Lynda.

"You've got to remember that I was also a civil rights student leader," Owen noted. "So if my name wasn't in the paper associated with Glass, my name was in the paper because I was involved in civil rights things not associated with Glass. And so, there was always that dynamic tension among my support group—"

"Who do you think you are," I offered.

"I'm a cause célèbre. 'How do we really relate to that?' You've still got all of that competition going on."

"Peer pressure," I offered. Upon reflection, however, I now believe Owen was not quoting all of Dunbar's A Track students when he said, "How do we really relate to that?" I think he was referring to Dunbar's young men. Deprived of his former male classmates' companionship, then subjected to their wariness, jealousy, and their adolescent need to one-up each other when he returned to his own community, Owen Cardwell's experience at Glass, as one of precious few African American males for four years (George Jackson, now Dr.

George Jackson, joined Owen in the fall of 1963), must have been particularly lonely and painful.

The differences between Lynda Woodruff's and Owen Cardwell's experience at their new high school became exceptionally clear when examining that all-important feature of high-school culture: sports. "In the context of predominantly White schools...Black boys may enjoy a degree of social success, particularly if they are athletically talented," notes Dr. Beverly Tatum.

"A lot of the dynamics took place in the sports arena because, as you probably remember, Glass had a pretty big football team," Owen recalled. "By that I mean, they had a lot of people trying out. So I tried out for the football team, and there were about sixty of us trying out." He named other classmates who'd vied for the chance to play. "I was a better player but what happened was, they had enough for five, full backfields in the trial. They would keep me in at every backfield until they just wore me down. So finally I quit and told my father that [the football coach] had cut me from the team."

He would say more on the lasting effects of this incident later.

For Lynda Woodruff, other arenas, female in nature, provided the same heartbreak: "The whole social culture, as you well know from your time there at E. C. Glass, was that if you were not a cheerleader, you were nothing."

Needless to say, although exceptionally attractive and athletic, Lynda Woodruff was not invited to join the cheerleading squad. Nor did she join any clubs, the other status symbol for females at the all-White school. "We weren't allowed to," she remembers with indignation.

Of course, when discussing both race *and* gender, Owen "being the only guy" was also potentially dangerous. "They didn't ask me who I was bringing to prom," Lynda Woodruff pointed out. "They didn't care. They wanted to know who he was bringing to prom. Because they didn't want it to be one of his White female classmates."

"So who did you bring?" I asked.

"I don't remember who I took," he replied. "Because, you see, Junior Ring Dance was a thing at Glass. That was not the case at Dunbar. The Senior Prom was the big emphasis. The only thing that I remember around that time was that Gail Thompson was at Amherst County High School. She had integrated Amherst County High School. And I was Gail's date for their Junior Ring Dance."

"So there was a little exchange?" I asked.

"Yeah, within the group of Negro desegregators," Lynda chimed in. "David Young had integrated Holy Cross. And he was my date."

After recalling some of those other "Negro desegregators," Lynda Woodruff reflected on another aspect of socialization at Glass. "Everything was a first. There was no recipe for us. There was no set of directions. How did we know what a Junior Ring Dance was? How did we know what a Senior Day was?"

"Those were totally outside of our cultural experience," Owen commented.

"And nobody to tell us," Dr. Woodruff added.

Georgia Barksdale, re-entering the room, reminded her daughter and Owen of the party they'd attended just before their arrival at Glass.

"We didn't see those kids after that," Lynda replied. "That was an isolated thing."

"They might not see you—" Georgia began.

"But that's part of the problem," Lynda countered. "We had no orientation."

"I know that."

"Then what's your point?"

"My point was that they weren't racists."

"Oh, please! You've got to be kidding!"

Georgia continued, calmly. "The point that was made at the party was [my senior classmates] didn't want to participate or maybe be with you because they would be ostracized—"

"Mother, some of the most racist kids in E. C. Glass were at that party!" And Lynda named one of my classmates, daughter of a prominent 03-er, someone I'd known well.

Listening to this exchange, now, and my own recorded chuckle as Lynda and Georgia argued, I realize that in that moment, I was simply registering: Mother-Daughter Conflict—the sort of disagreement I know very well from painful personal experience.

I now hear so much more: I hear Georgia both as a loving, protective mother but also as the person who'd earlier invoked the name of Martin Luther King, Jr., i.e. "Martin Luther King didn't want [other Dunbar students to hear of the difficulties of desegregation]." In other words, I hear Georgia Barksdale not only as Lynda's mother but also spiritually grounded in the civil rights movement, able to forgive. "Dr. King would often say that we've got to love people no matter what." I hear Lynda Woodruff's painful memories of that time and her overpowering sense that no one, not even her loving mother, can understand what she and Owen experienced. And I hear that as an African American woman, Lynda Woodruff's assessment of certain E. C. Glass students reveals an ugly side to my former classmates that I, naturally, never saw, never suspected.

"In retrospect, though, and really—I kind of made this point in class today [Reverend Cardwell was, at the time, pursuing a Ph.D. at Liberty University]—retrospect's all we have right now. I believe there were pragmatic racists and ideological racists and I have less problem with the pragmatic racist than I do the ideological one," asserted Owen. [Mary Spottswood Payne's] son became a friend of mine in my senior year. That was an evolving process... Adin Thayer [Short-skirted Pam Thayer's younger sister] and Jill Levin took real risks in befriending us."

When GC neglected to register Owen and Lynda for the SATs, Connie Moore, a classmate and friend, got them the necessary information. "She was 'White Trash,' they used to say," Owen recalled.

"Because she was our friend," Lynda rejoined. "They ostracized her all over the place."

After the pair recalled the handful of White classmates who had been their friends, Owen again mentioned his contributions to Lynchburg's civil rights movement.

"The other thing that you have to understand that was taking place at that time is that not only was I the only male, but I was also a political activist," he pointed out. "Which did not endear me. I was the president of the junior chapter of S.N.C.C. [Student Nonviolent Coordinating Committee] here in the city. And so, I was arrested in Danville; I led sit-in demonstrations here in the city.

"I got involved with S.N.C.C. because of Virgil. See, Virgil's presence here and his affiliation with Martin King brought us a lot of exposure in the whole civil rights strategy.

"I never will forget when we strategized in the basement of Diamond Hill [Baptist Church] to integrate S & W Cafeteria. White students were brought in from Philadelphia to act as look-outs for us. They went into S & W Cafeteria, we parked down the hill—S & W was out in Pittman Plaza [an early Lynchburg mall]—we parked down the hill, White kids came to the public telephone booth right out front of the S & W, called us, we ran up the hill, went into the cafeteria, and were seated before they could call the police or anything. And we sat at the table with the White kids that were plants, and Brenda [Hughes] even did something that was very symbolic. She ate watermelon off the plate with a kid. While we were sitting there, they had the police to come in. They made an announcement that they were closing the cafeteria.

"The next morning, Whirlwind Johnson, who was on the Bi-Racial Commission at that time—the Bi-Racial Commission had been called in—and the next day, they made an announcement that they were integrating S & W Cafeteria. But we didn't get any credit for what we had done the day before."

"Oh, right, the Bi-Racial Committee took credit," Lynda Woodruff remembered.

"We also did sit-ins at the Warner Theater and the Paramount Theater. The summer of my junior year, we were very, very active."

"I tended to be really, really, really isolated in my political knowledge," said Lynda Woodruff, again making clear the differences between her experiences and Owen's.

"...But go back before we went to Glass," she suggested. "The other thing—it wasn't even in John Lewis's book. [We'd talked about *Walking with the Wind* before the interview.] But they are finally documenting the Prince Edward County. I've seen two snippets last year, in 2001, about Prince Edward's school system. I am telling you, that has been one of the most buried, nasty secrets of the civil rights movement. And it was not exposed."

"They [Prince Edward County, VA, officials] shut down the schools rather than integrate," I remembered.

"There's a generation your age, your class—" Lynda began.

"—that got no education," Owen completed.

"Unless you could pay for it," I said.

"No, no, no," corrected Lynda. "If you were Black, there was no place to buy it. Only the White kids got an education. There was no 'Pay For It,' they had to ship them out to relatives all over the country, all over the state."

"Well, the Black churches did take them in," added Owen.

"Virgil Wood had that whole picnic. I'll never forget. It was right after we had heard the decision that we were going to Glass. The same time, Virgil had busloads of kids come up from Prince Edward County. And so I remember feeling—that whole experience of being with those children and knowing what happened in Prince Edward, then knowing that the next year, January, I feared we would have the same thing."

Can you imagine that thirteen-year-old girl's terror that she might be somehow responsible for an entire school system shutting down?

"Edna Ross's mother kept four people from Prince Edward," Lynda recalled. "So [Lynchburg] people who had family took these people in. Those are the people our age. My question for forty years has been, What happened to the kids who were due to go to kindergarten? How long were the schools—I never recall them reopening!"

"They didn't," joked Reverend Cardwell. (Prince Edward's African American students returned to school four years later, due to the Supreme Court's *Griffin versus County School Board*.)

"Thank you. I had no idea. You have no history on this," Dr. Woodruff concluded.

You have no history on this. As I had just made clear with my "Unless you could pay for it," statement, I indeed knew very little about Prince Edward County; I'd never even heard of "massive resistance." (Some might wonder, given my lack of information regarding Virginia history during the civil rights era, why I even had the nerve to interview Lynda and Owen!) But I did have history of sorts about Prince Edward.

My story begins in the summer of 1961, soon after Lynda and Owen had requested to be transferred from Dunbar to Glass. Like others of my race and class, I had spent the summer between my junior and senior year of high school looking at colleges. Not surprisingly, given my family's New England roots and my eagerness to get out of the South, all the schools I considered were located in the northeast.

At the very beginning of one college interview on some leafy New England campus, a tweedy college-admissions man, noticing my Virginia address, looked at me with some concern. "Are you going to school?" he asked. "Is your school open?"

"That's just in Prince Edward," I replied.

"Tell me about it," he urged. So I, aware—and grateful—that I was back in the North where the subject of segregation could at least be discussed, told that tweedy man what I knew of Prince Edward County, a place which in my adolescent world view, was far, far away from Lynchburg (although, in reality, it was very near). I chose my words carefully, I remember. What little I knew about Prince Edward was what I had read in Lynchburg's newspapers, owned by the staunchly segregationist Glass family. So I was careful not to put a southern spin on what I said.

"He thought I wasn't going to school!" I reported incredulously to my parents after the interview.

"He just wanted to hear how you present information," my father explained. "Of course he knows you're going to school!"

My father's analysis of that college admissions person's question could be filed under the heading of Things Privileged People Just *Know* and Pass On To Their Privileged Children. But what happens when parents *don't* know how to negotiate the complicated college-admissions process? If they're lucky, like Lynda and Owen had been, another adult—their "White Trash" classmate's mother—steps in. Then, as now, however, it seems too much to expect a high school guidance counselor to actually guide the application process. Connie Moore's mother, herself a college professor, initially became involved because GC had withheld vital information from Lynda and Owen.

I asked Lynda and Owen a question I'd been waiting to ask: "Did you ever feel that your presence in E. C. Glass meant that people were actually talking and learning from one another?"

"No way did that happen!" Lynda responded heatedly. *"We* learned. I think they actively tried not to." She paused. "Let me back off. That's rather adamant."

"Going back to the here and now," offered Owen, "I don't think that there was a sense among the White community that this was going any further than it did. And so there was no need—"

"That you two were going to be it?" I suggested.

"Well, not so much that us two would be it, or us four would be it," began Owen Cardwell, "but that there would be no wholesale—"

"Let me tell you—" his co-desegregator began.

"Can I finish?"

"Hmm," Dr. Woodruff assented.

"Thank you," he replied.

"But hurry up about it, for God's sake," she added. And then they laughed. There is an easy, loving, brother and sister, connected feeling between Reverend Cardwell and Dr. Woodruff. And a deeply felt respect.

Owen proceeded. "I don't think there was any sense that there would be any wholesale application, that this was more or less an experiment. Yeah, they might have to tolerate trickling-in, but there was no abject need on their part to examine the experience at all because there was no real threat."

"This too shall pass," offered Lynda.

"There! There was no real threat," Owen repeated.

And then it was Lynda Woodruff's turn. "Now, go back to what I said to you a minute ago. They programmed our failure. Why the civil rights leaders allowed a judgment to send people into a school in January, thirty-two chapters behind in Latin? They programmed that there would be no need to address this issue. They figured we would flunk and run."

Owen addressed his next remark to Lynda: "Well, you ask the question, Why did the Black leaders allow that? I asked Wyatt Walker just this past summer—"

Sheepishly, I asked who he was.

"Famous Black preacher," answered Lynda.

"He was also one of Martin Luther King's lieutenants," Owen offered.

" 'You can take my drum, but you cannot take my beat,' " Dr. Woodruff quoted.

"He was pastoring in Petersburg [Virginia] at the time, by the way," Owen continued. "I asked Wyatt, 'Why didn't you all, as civil rights leaders, train the next generation?' He said, 'Owen, we were so much more wildly successful, beyond our dreams, that we didn't recognize the need for it.' "

"That's right," Lynda pronounced.

"And so," Owen continued, "I think that when she asked the question, 'Why did the Black leadership allow that?' I think that even Virgil—"

"—still thinks it was successful," his co-desegregator offered.

"Yeah! It was beyond their wildest imagination that they would ever get this really done. Even though they were going to fight the good fight. That they took what was given to them," Owen concluded. These last words were pronounced almost as though they'd been italicized or underlined. So perhaps the Richmond pastor's pronouncement should be repeated: They, the Black civil rights leaders of the early sixties, took what was given to them.

"See," he continued, "I have questioned—"

"And they didn't look beyond," Georgia offered from the kitchen.

"And they didn't look beyond," Owen Cardwell agreed. "I have questioned for years, whenever the question arises, always around Martin Luther King's birthday, and Black History Month, I get these calls from these reporters for interviews and everything. They've asked the question every year, 'Would you do it again?' And I've grown to say, having seen the result: no. I would never subject myself—and this is part of what I'm going to say tomorrow night—I would never put myself in that position. Because, I think, though I understand what Wyatt Walker was saying, *I* think that we were sold a bill of goods. I think that all along, we fought [for] integration, though the discussion was desegregation. We settled for desegregation."

Lynda Woodruff joined him as they both declared, "Never got integration."

"The same thing is part of *my* presentation for tomorrow," Lynda continued, "because I'm looking back, looking around, looking forward…When I left Lynchburg to go to college, I was fine. Stay gone, come home, brief visit, gone again. I have never been a part of this community since 1965. Owen came home and worked. Owen came home and lived. Owen came home and married. Owen even pastored a church here. The closest I've come to coming back home was Danville. And that was—excuse me—damned close enough. And let me tell you why.

"I came home one summer; I can't even remember how many years ago. And one of my cousins, little cousins, was then at E. C. Glass. And she looked at me at a family funeral or something, and she says, 'Cousin Lynda, I've been just dying to meet you forever!' And she says, 'I'm surprised. You're really kind of nice.'

"And I looked to my left and I looked to my right and said, 'You talking to me?'

"And she says, 'Yeah.'

"I said, 'Where does that kind of comment come from?'

"She says, 'My teachers, my Black teachers at E. C. Glass that teach us Black History, say you and Owen ruined it for everybody!'

"That was the first time that I had even thought that thought. That somebody would think of the whole desegregation experience as negative. Or hurtful to somebody. We didn't do it to hurt anybody!…They were actually teaching kids at E. C. Glass, in the eighties this was, that the desegregation of E. C. Glass was bad, detrimental; the reason that all of those young kids at that time were failing and not being successful was the fault of one Owen Cardwell and Lynda Woodruff.

"For the first time in my recent history and memory, I was absolutely speechless! I was flabbergasted. And I kept up a relationship with that kid; I have her letters still."

"Why did they come to that conclusion?" Owen questioned. But then he suggested, "You're playing into what I just said."

"Exactly," Lynda replied.

"Okay. I agree with that. I agree with that from that vantage point. My image, just now, was that of Rodney King asking, 'Can't we just get along?' And I want to say, 'Hell, no, Nigger! We can't just get along! Don't you understand what's happening to you? You're being beat to death in the streets, here!'

"We can't get along until we have an understanding that we're equals at the table," Reverend Cardwell concluded.

◆

Forty years after he and Lynda desegregated E. C. Glass, and five months after the attacks on the World Trade Center and the Pentagon, Owen Cardwell, still yearning for that equality at that table, reflected on the still-yawning chasm between Black and White America.

"To show you how far apart we are in terms of our world view, I don't hear a whole lot of Black folks reminiscing or talking about 9/11. I see White folks having memorials, even now. Reliving it."

"When is somebody going to ask," Lynda queried, "what cultural, ethnic, and racial difference is there in this country to 9/11? I have been waiting for someone to ask me."

She then related a story of being confronted by three of her White college students for not flying "our nation's flag" after September 11.

"Wasn't that tragic?" she had said to the trio. "And they'd said, 'You're being sarcastic.'

"No, I'm not," she told them. "But I also think slavery was tragic. I also think Little Big Horn was tragic. I also think it was tragic when they rounded up the Japanese after Pearl Harbor. I also think it was tragic—and I named them about five major tragedies, and then counted the numbers up. And it came to more than five thousand. How 'bout to the power of a hundred? How about five-hundred million when you add them all up?

"...Osama Bin Laden ain't never called me 'Nigger,' " she declared. "I get called 'Nigger' every day on my job! Oh, yes."

Something occurred to her: "Did you ever read *Black Like Me*?" she asked me. I had.

"[John Howard] Griffin?" Reverend Cardwell asked.

"Griffin," Professor Woodruff affirmed. "I read it again. Had my whole class read it last year. They hate my guts for making them read it. A whole bunch [however] wrote me little thank-you notes: 'Thank you. Now I understand.' So if it takes somebody White, painting themselves Black, to help you understand, have *at* it. Read it five more times. I've been telling you for years but you can't hear me."

"There's a thing in Griffin called the hate stare," Lynda continued. "Get that every day I can breathe! What do I do with it? What do you think I do with it?"

"You are a serious Type A personality," Reverend Cardwell observed, laughing.

"Not only that, I like myself!" she rejoined. "Ph.D., full professor, old, getting ready to retire; there is nothing about their hate stares that can unnerve me.

"That's what E. C. Glass did for me. I learned, by the second twenty-ninth, by February twenty-ninth, to let all that roll. If I had to react to racism, if I could have been troubled by a hate stare, we wouldn't be sitting here talking to you."

"Right," added Reverend Cardwell, softly.

"And think back to that developmental contact of a thirteen year old."

"Oh, I have been thinking about that," I said. I was remembering, for example, Dr. Tatum's observation: "Researchers have found that adolescents of color are more likely to be actively engaged in an exploration of their racial or ethnic identity than are White students."

"On a very personal level," Reverend Cardwell offered, "over the years, I've had to ask myself—for a long time, I've had a hard time completing anything. I really didn't want to finish Glass. I had an opportunity—Father Teeter had, through his church connection, made an offer to my father to [help me] go to Andover [Phillips Academy]."

"Oh, that's right!" Lynda was reminded.

"I had a full scholarship," he continued. "My father told me I couldn't go. That I had to finish what I started at Glass."

"I was happy for him," Lynda Woodruff commented. "But I would have had a nervous breakdown if he'd bailed on me!"

"And so for a long time, I couldn't finish anything. And I've always wondered whether my experience at Glass had anything to do with that."

"Oh, I'm sure," Lynda Woodruff pronounced.

"I finished because I couldn't go to Phillips, and then, when I graduated from Glass, I had scholarship offers to Oberlin, to Wittenberg—" There were other prestigious schools but he couldn't recall them. "I do remember Oberlin and Wittenberg because I seriously considered those because of their history. But I made a conscious choice to go to Hampton University."

"Why?" I asked.

"I didn't want to have anything to do with White folks."

"It's all Black," Dr. Woodruff reminded me.

"I wanted to have socialization as part of my college experience," he spelled out for me. Deprived of interaction with his peers, particularly with other young African American males, the eighteen-year old Owen Cardwell sought the much-needed companionship and identity-exploration Dr. Tatum described.

"I got accepted in all kinds of places in the South," Lynda Woodruff explained. "And I wanted the heck out of the South. So I ran to Ohio. It was Connie Moore's mother, Ellen Moore, who introduced me to Case Western Reserve...But my analysis of the thing for Owen; I support him completely in what he's saying. I would have the same doubt [re identity].

"Now, remember, you're talking, of course, male and female personalities, egos. Owen hasn't said it to you, probably. I will say it to you. Owen's IQ is in the genius range. He and a couple of other people in Lynchburg were the highest scorers in the history of Lynchburg public education."

"I did not know that," I said, impressed. But, really, not surprised.

"The class of '65 was the largest class in the history of Lynchburg public education," Lynda went on. "And it has not, yet, been topped according to a little paper I got from E. C. Glass."

"Class of '65 had the highest number of Merit Scholars," Owen added.

"Highest number of Merit Scholars...produced the largest numbers of Ph.Ds, MDs, all these things." Dr. Woodruff continued. "My thing is: ordinary person over here [i.e., herself], and a family of college-educated professionals [i.e. Owen], over there. To have that whole self-esteem piece, that whole 'Who do I think I am?' piece constantly eroded, on a daily basis at E. C. Glass, it's no wonder. 'What are you finishing for?' 'Why should I finish?'

"The thing that I think saved me is because I didn't go to a Black school, I saw an analysis, so to speak, of the White experience. By the time I got to a White campus, up North, with a bunch of other kids like me, who had desegregated schools all over the South, we then had some support. We had each other to run it by. Owen never had that experience, I don't think."

"No," he replied. "And on top of that—"

"We had Black professors who then chose to do research on the subject," she interjected.

Remembering that her colleague was now in a doctoral program, and taking courses in psychology and sociology, she became excited: "I can't wait for you to get all down in 'the literature' so we can argue some more! About that, too!"

But even before Owen's "getting down in the literature," he had already developed a theory as to why, forty years later, their recollections so often differed: "I've come to the conclusion that part of the reason why Lynda remembers so much of the details and I don't," Owen began, "also has to do with how we would probably score on a DISC Personality Indicator." Lynda, they both agreed, could be classified as a "Dominator" whereas Owen was "An Influencer."

"What was going on at E. C. Glass with me was not as important to me, at the time, as the Big-Picture political arena."

"And the opposite with me," Lynda declared. "I was more focused on day-to-day experience. That's another issue that really unnerves me. Because when people want to report on the E. C. Glass experience, they lump us as if we were not individual, concrete human beings."

Circling back to the What Glass Did To Me Theme, Lynda Woodruff declared, "I'm not looking to defend my personality. I've got all kinds of flaws. I'm angry. I'm defensive. I'm combative. I interrupt. I speak; I'm going to be heard. You're going to hear it, whether you want to or not. And if you don't want to hear it, I'm going to write it to you. The whole nine yards. How much of that is E. C. Glass?"

At another point during the interview, however, in spite of the hardships, the humiliations, the personal sacrifices and the pain the two firsts had so poignantly described, Lynda made this ringing statement: "We advanced the race light years!" she declared.

✦

As the first two Negro desegregators, Lynda Woodruff and Owen Cardwell shared another immediate, potentially dangerous, day-to-day concern: Whom could they trust within the walls of E. C. Glass? What they discovered was not unexpected: "There was a [Black] janitor that for the life of me—I want to say 'Otis?'—I can't remember. But anyway, there was one janitor that if we were in the hall, that man started brooming down the hall. We were walking someplace, he was pushing that mop, coming right on by! To my knowledge, he never, ever [spoke]. I could not describe his voice to you.

"We did not have any clue as to who we could or could not trust."

The one Glass person Lynda Woodruff remembered with tears in her eyes, from her very first day at E. C. Glass, was a Black cafeteria worker by the name of Thelma Campbell.

"The thing that was just so remarkable was the stuff we didn't know," she began. "Now, remember, coming from Dunbar, very organized, very small, everybody in that school knew each other both in school and in the community. We get dropped into an ocean of twenty-six hundred students, a hundred-some faculty, maybe? I don't know."

"Actually, there were thirty-two hundred kids," Reverend Cardwell corrected her.

"Thirty-two hundred kids, right," she agreed. "Anyhow, that first day, did we know there were two cafeterias? No!...I was not where you [two] were. I was in the other cafeteria, terrified, because I couldn't find him: 'My God, did he turn White between first period and fourth period?' "

"I crossed over!" her co-desegregator joked.

" 'Did he leave me, here? Has he gone home? Did somebody hurt him?' I panicked when I couldn't find Owen. And, of course, the newspaper says, 'Everything went just perfectly fine.' Well, that was the biggest lie!

"I was in the very back of the line in Cafeteria Two; he was over there with you, making a scene in Cafeteria One."

"Not much of a scene," I noted.

"When that line got closer to the door to go in," Dr. Woodruff continued, "I looked in there, and for the first time in my E. C. Glass career, I found my survival rope. Her name was Thelma Campbell."

"Right," Reverend Cardwell added, well, reverently.

"And she looked at me, and I guess I had to have been crying at the time. Tears, but silently suffering. When I got into the line, she had—I remember it clearly: White lady, nice, little lady with this handkerchief and her nametag on it. Said 'Supervisor' on it—so Thelma's supervisor was standing on her left arm and the dietetics director was standing on her right arm [inside the kitchen where food was served]. Well, everybody was where they could see the two Negroes! [Thelma] was trying to communicate to me that Owen was safe and in the next cafeteria. Except I didn't know what she was saying! She kept doing the head thing [gesturing with her head towards the other cafeteria]. Because I didn't know there were two cafeterias. So I thought Thelma had a tic. Some sort of neurological disorder or something! But she finally got an excuse to come out [from the kitchen area to the area with tables and chairs] under the pretense of picking up ketchup bottles or whatever, and she says, 'Hi, child, you okay?'

"I said, 'Fine.'

"She says, 'Owen's over in the other cafeteria. He's okay.' And that's when I realized there were two cafeterias and that's where Owen was. So that calmed me down."

Later Lynda was to say: "I don't believe—and maybe I'm wrong—that people would even have the capacity to feel the fear of me walking in that cafeteria and not finding Owen. To feel the fear of having to be dragged in [to GC's office for the shortness of her kilt.] Am I going to get expelled? The fear, the embarrassment, the humiliation."

A thirteen-year-old girl silently crying. A young man worn out from his never-ending stint on a football field. Nasty, race-baiting, unsigned cards on Valentine's Day. Threatening phone calls night after night. Constantly being called "Nigger" in the hall. Boxes of sanitary napkins delivered to the Barksdale home day after day. Could Dr. Woodruff be right? Can none of us understand those teenagers' fear, their humiliation, their embarrassment?

Could I? As painful as it is to admit, it is clear from listening to my voice and my questions on these tapes, that on some level I seemed to have been under the impression that the three of us were reminiscing about our E. C. Glass experience while standing at a reunion party, gin and tonics in hand! It would take more time before I was able to let Lynda and Owen's words grow, breathe, and act in me.

✦

The next evening, just before Lynda Woodruff and Owen Cardwell were to give their keynote speeches, Hermina Hendricks, Randolph-Macon's director of Multicultural Services, hosted a dinner in the pair's honor in one of the college's private, gracious, gently lit dining rooms. The two honored guests, Georgia and Ed Barksdale, a racially mixed group of student representatives, and I were treated to a delicious dinner served, I noticed, by an all-White waitstaff.

Hermina Hendricks, a brisk and attractive woman and a Dunbar High graduate, sat at one end of our long, food-laden table. Somehow, I ended up seated at the opposite end. During a lull in the conversation, she looked down the length of the table at me.

"Patricia!" she said loudly, as if she'd just noticed my presence. "Why are you here?"

Already feeling awkward by my place-of-honor seating, I was, at first, unsure how to answer. But then I was "moved" as Quakers say, to tell the E. C. Glass cafeteria story, the same story I'd told to Darrell Laurant a couple of years before, the same story I've been telling in varied settings for over forty years. But that evening, something remarkable happened, probably because so many of those listening to my story were college students. My hackneyed tale took on a freshness, a vitality, and a significance from those young women's deep, attentive listening.

"We thought she was another guilty White woman when we first met her," Owen informed the gathering.

A couple of times the night before, Lynda and Owen had touched upon the Town/Gown relationship between Randolph-Macon and the segregated Lynchburg they'd known. As I watched the two of them being fussed over at dinner, heard the enthusiastic applause, saw the standing ovation and then observed lines of R-MWC students waiting afterward to shake their hands—some students asked for their autographs—I was aware that even in this moment of triumph for Dr. Woodruff and Reverend Cardwell, there were "old pieces of pain." Seeing them graciously interact with the crowd, it occurred to me how often people of color in this country bring a painful story, a history, an oft-repeated tale in their community "to the table."

✦

Houston Memorial Chapel, a large, modern, wood-paneled space, was filled to near-capacity. Among those seated in the audience were Randolph-Macon students, members of Lynchburg's African American community, Barksdale and Cardwell family members, and Lynda and Owen's former teachers, including their Sunday school teachers. (Owen was raised Baptist, Lynda became an Episcopalian in high school.)

Before launching into her speech, Dr. Woodruff commented on a news report she'd heard in the Atlanta airport on her way to Lynchburg:

"Two sixteen-year-old students had been shot, wounded, at what high school, folks? Martin Luther King High School in Manhattan. I hung my head, I couldn't believe it. I said, 'What is this? A message? Am I supposed to get something, here?' Is this ironical? Or is this just plain stupid? It's his birthday, for crying out loud. And someone has the nerve to shoot up a school on Dr. King's birthday!

"The Dr. King that Owen and I met in 1962. The Dr. King that came to Lynchburg to hold our hands, if you will, to tell us everything was going to be all right. We didn't believe it, but he told us everything was going to be all right. He assured us that non-violence was the way. Never mind my temper! He begged us to comply with what had been prescribed by the Southern Christian Leadership Conference.

"In 1962, there were no cell phones. Oh, wouldn't it have been nice, though, if we could have gone off to a corner and dialed Martin Luther King and say, 'Yo, Dr. King! We in trouble, here!'...

"There was no 911 in Lynchburg in 1962. So if there had been an emergency, what 911 would we have dialed? We didn't even have emergency exits at Glass. The emergency exits got put up after we arrived."

The chapel audience roared with laughter.

"Now, that was not supposed to be funny," she commented.

"We had bomb threats. Every other day or so, sometimes twice a day, we had to shuffle out of our classes and into the gymnasium while the cops came from downtown Lynchburg to look for bombs. We had no bomb-sniffing dogs, either."

I remember those sessions in the gymnasium. Glass cheerleaders, not in uniform, and probably terrified (Had the gymnasium already been searched? Did anyone really know?), with a notable lack of enthusiasm or pep, perfunctorily led all of us in football and basketball cheers: "With an L, with a Y with a L-Y-N, with an L-Y-N-C-H. With a B, with a U, with a B-U-R, with a B-U-R-G-H [sic]. Lynchburg, Lynchburg, fight 'em, fight 'em, fight 'em, big blue and white!" No one ever said these bomb scares were because of Lynda and Owen. No one had to.

"We crossed that threshold on January twenty-ninth, and despite the strength of the community, the power of our resolve, the great civil rights movement, there was one thing that was crystal-clear to us then. And that was 'Hello, Brother. We never liked each other before, we gonna fall in love today.' We knew clearly that we were alone...

"...I can't stop grieving over the fact that in the year 2002, we're still talking about the need for diversity, the need to learn to know each other, the need to be comrades. We've got to move on, guys, we've got to get to the doing part. We've been thinking about studying the problem of our existence, now, for way-forty-years too long…

"Several years ago, I was invited to give a Martin King presentation at an elementary school in Georgia…I never taught in the lower grades so I was anxious and I asked a first-grade teacher how to do this and she told me, 'Do Show and Tell.' So I took my favorite picture of Martin Luther King to the Martin Luther King Day at the elementary school. Very nervous, I held up the picture and said, 'Who is this person?' In unison, these children, in a predominantly Black school, said, 'O.J. Simpson.'

"Now, I'm going to get real serious with you. That was not funny. I was absolutely mortified. We have work to do. That story is only to say we do have a picture. There's a tremendous challenge ahead of us and we must rise to that challenge in the next forty years."

After praising the contributions Randolph-Macon women "of grit and salt and strength and power" had made and would continue to make towards civil rights, Dr. Woodruff concluded: "It is time, I'm looking forward to it, and Owen, you've got eight minutes."

A spirited rendition of "America the Beautiful," performed by The Rivermont Baptist Church Mass Choir, followed Lynda's speech. When the African American soloist, Reverend Doctor James Cobbs, sang "undimmed by human tears," the chapel crowd roared. Maybe those words should be the title of this book, I thought, deeply moved.

Owen began his eight minutes by first thanking Reverend Cobbs: "You've helped me to reflect on what really got Lynda and me over, in the course of helping to desegregate the schools, here in Lynchburg…

"When people ask me, 'Would you do it again?' one of the things that comes to my mind is a passage from Scripture that says, 'Where your treasure is, there will be your heart, also.' Forty years later, I look around and I ask: Where are our hearts? What's up with this?

"The average annual cost to incarcerate a juvenile in Virginia is approximately sixty-thousand dollars. There is not one school district in America that spends one-fifth of that amount in per-pupil allocations to educate. Where are our hearts? And what's up with that?

"African American males are three times more likely to be in jail than in college. A recent California study showed that 66 percent of ninth graders are expected to graduate from high school. I don't think that is very far from the mark around the country. What that means is this: If you have three children, one of them won't graduate from high school. What's up with that?

"In Henrico County where my grandchildren go to school, we had an experience with the school system. One of my grandsons has a speech impediment, therefore, lacking services for him, they put him in special education. Each year, we had to do what is called an IEP [Individualized Education Plan]. And because of his stuttering problem, I believe that he had some early traumas in his educational process when he would try to answer questions and he was embarrassed. So learning is difficult for him.

"At our last IEP session, they were trying to figure out a way to provide him with more special-educational services. The only category that they figured that he could fit into to receive special education services was ADHD [Attention-deficit, hyperactive disorder]. I said, 'You are not doing that to my grandson.' "

"That's right," shouted a few people in the audience.

"Because what they didn't know is," Reverend Cardwell continued, "they had their worst nightmare sitting in front of them: An educated Negro who understood the system."

The audience applauded enthusiastically.

"So my wife called Henrico County schools and asked them if they had any data to tell us how many African American males were in special education in Henrico County. The woman on the other end of the phone wanted to know why she needed the information. My wife said, 'Because I'm a taxpayer. Is it a secret?'

"When they sent us the data, we discovered that although African American males only make up 20 percent of the school district, they made up 27 percent of those in special education. What's up with that?

"...It seems to me that public agencies, academia, business, the public schools, the community are at cross-purposes from each other. To paraphrase: It takes a village to educate a child. Education is a community responsibility. And we have abdicated that responsibility to the public schools. Teachers used to be more than classroom technicians. It scares me, it frightens me when I see the new education bill pass. When Standards of Learning testing is going to be the litmus test for education for our children [More on this Virginia "high stakes" test later]. It frightens me because, even here in Virginia, we're teaching our kids to take tests and not educating our children. Classroom experience has been relegated to learning [how] to raise the pupils' test scores.

"...In every community in America, we need to reassess what we are allowing to happen to our children...

"...An assistant principal right here in the city of Lynchburg [told me] how she couldn't get parents to come to PTA meetings and how parents are not interested in the education of their children.

"And I said to her, 'Rather than to have working parents and single parents choose between work and PTA, or just getting some needed rest, and then condemn those parents for lack of interest in their child, why not have PTA at the local church after the morning service and let the church's hospitality committee serve lunch?' Why are we making it so inconvenient for a family to participate in the educational process of their children?

"I'm going to challenge my hometown. We're trying to do this all over America. For every dollar spent in public education, we need to raise ten cents from the community so that every child in a school district that needs after-school care can receive it. We need to take back the education of our children. Boston financial institutions led the business community in the Boston Partnership with the Boston Ministerial Alliance and they raised twenty-three million dollars. They opened the doors of churches after school to provide after-school care and tutorial support, homework support, for any child in Boston that wants it.

"When I look at what we invested forty years ago, and I look at the payoff today, I have got to ask the question: What's up with that?"

Owen Cardwell's oft-repeated question was answered by a round of applause. He probably should have concluded his remarks then, as depressing as that ending was. He chose, however, to read an e-mail he recently received concerning September 11 and the question, 'How could God have let something like this happen?'

The response, written by evangelist Billy Graham's daughter, Anne, began: "I believe God is deeply sad about this just as we are. But for years we have been telling God to get out of our schools…" And while a few people in the audience responded favorably to these sentiments, I thought I detected a chill among the Randolph-Macon students seated near me which became more pronounced when Reverend Cardwell quoted Anne Graham's mean-spirited swipe at Doctor Spock and her Religious-Right views on abortion.

Registering my disappointment that Owen had chosen to read this e-mail, I realized that I'd shifted locations a little. Reverend Owen C. Cardwell, the "skinny black kid in the corner," the man whose voice had made me cry the first time I had heard it, the man I had idolized from the moment he'd sung "If They Told The Story of My Life" at his ministerial banquet, had become human, less than perfect in my eyes: a person.

NOTES: Sinking Down

p. 83. "Small blue sedan."
"Small? An Oldsmobile?" commented Dr. Woodruff dryly, years later.

p. 83. "Firsts":
"There's this huge gap, and so even if there are a few folks that were or are able to break through, there are still only those few. Our generation has replaced "firsts" with "onlys;" the only black person in such and such position. I'm the only black writer at *Fortune* magazine, and I shouldn't be in 2005."

(Cora Daniels, quoted in *Uncle Tom or New Negro: African Americans Reflect on Booker T. Washington and Up From Slavery 100 Years Later*, by Rebecca Carroll, Harlem Moon, NY, 2006, p. 102)

p. 84. "They published our IQs…"

Ironically, one of the most controversial writers on the volatile subject of African American intelligence testing, Audrey Shuey, taught at the same college that would honor Lynda and Owen many years later. A Randolph-Macon Woman's College professor, Dr. Shuey published *The Testing of Negro Intelligence* in 1958. After carefully presenting her testing methods and results—she tested "Racial Hybrids" and "Deviates" as well as African American elementary and high school children, among others—the Randolph-Macon professor concluded her lengthy book with the statement that her testing results "inevitably point to the presence of native differences between Negroes and whites as determined by intelligence tests." Branded a racist, "a segregationist scientist" and her book "the bible" for those anthropologists, biologists, psychologists, and sociologists who firmly believed that there was a fundamental disparity between White and Black intelligence, Shuey was and continues to be reviled. In the years following the publication of her controversial book, many scientists, including Noam Chomsky and Stephen Jay Gould, have strongly disputed the Randolph-Macon professor's findings.

p. 85. Olivet Thaxton (from "No Matter How Long," p. 51)

In 1960, soon after one of Lynchburg's first civil rights demonstrations, when a racially mixed group of college students had been arrested for a sit-in at Patterson Drug Store, Olivet C. Thaxton, owner of a hauling business and a charter member of the Lynchburg Improvement Association, lost his contract with the downtown drugstore.

"[Mr. Patterson] told me why he'd fired me," the African American entrepreneur explained to O. C. Cardwell. "As you know, I had a contract to do hauling for him and several of his stores once a week and these sit-inners sat in his drugstore. They locked them up and so they had a mass meeting to raise money. Someone called me up and asked me to assist in lifting the offering at Court Street Baptist Church. I went up to assist in lifting the offering. The next day, Mr. Patterson called me and wanted me to see him. He wanted to talk to me and I went down to his place of business and he told me that someone told him that I was working harder against him than for him. He fired me right there on the spot, right then."

p. 85. Economic pressures on students' parents:

In a December 6, 2000, interview with Henry Heil, Brenda Hughes Andrews talked about her mother, Mabel's, livelihood:

"Mabel Hughs [sic] worked as a domestic for a white Lynchburg family. According to her daughter, that family never once complained or insinuated that her mother's job was in jeopardy due to her involvement in the school desegregation issue, nor was she concerned. Like Fred Harris [Crystabel Harris's father] before, Mabel Hughs cared more that her daughter obtained access to quality education than she did about losing her domestic work."

p. 86. Mine workers:

The *Lynchburg News* reported: "We are gratified to learn that one hundred and fifty negroes employed at the Wythe Iron Mines, all of whom voted the straight out radical ticket, were discharged on Tuesday by the owner of the works." *Negro in Virginia*, p. 254

p. 89. Lynchburg Training School

Lynchburg Training School was a state-run hospital for the developmentally delayed. A few months after Lynda and Owen began Glass, I volunteered there every week.

p. 92.

Beverly Tatum, *"Why Are All The Black Kids Sitting Together in the Cafeteria?"* (p. 58)

p. 94. "Dr. King would often say. . . "

John Lewis in his memoir, *Walking with the Wind: a Memoir of The Movement* (p. 78)

pp. 95. "The Bi-Racial Commission"

Referred to as the Bi-Racial Commission in O. C. Cardwell's "No Matter How Long," the name of Lynchburg's "United Nations to mediate across racial lines" was the Lynchburg Interracial Committee (Laurant, p. 121)

p. 95. Brenda Hughes

Brenda Hughes is now Brenda Andrews and the editor and publisher of *The New Journal and Guide,* one of the South's oldest African American newspapers.

p. 98. Guidance counselors:

As I had discovered at Allison's race forum, sometimes today's guidance counselors aren't much better. Chinese-American Mang, one of Allison's best friends, told the race-forum attendees how difficult the college application process had been for her. Although an excellent student and a strong candidate for any number of elite colleges, Mang's immigrant parents had not known where to begin. When Mang discovered that her overworked guidance counselor devoted her energies to non-AP-class students, Mang was forced to apply to colleges on her own.

"Because I'm Chinese, people always assume I'm good at math," Mang explained at the forum. And just *know* all about interviews, SATs, and financial aid.

You have no history on this. In a way, Lynda was right: Unexamined history, like an unexamined life, doesn't add up to much. The Things I *Do* Just Know are often informed by my race and class. When I heard Mang's story, I realized—again—how often I assume that other Americans' history, their stories, are the same as mine.

And the Things I Don't Know could fill a library. When I finally did my homework on massive resistance, I discovered that, actually, other Virginia communities—nearby Charlottesville, for one—had briefly closed their public schools rather than integrate. To my amazement, I also learned that the tweedy college-admissions man had actually asked me a pertinent question. Just a couple of years before I began the college application process, *all* the cities and towns of Virginia had been perilously close to locking their school doors.

p. 101. "In the eighties, this was."

During the eighties, of course, the Reagan Administration was systematically dismantling much of the progress gained during the civil rights era. The anger and frustration expressed by Glass's Black teachers towards Lynda and Owen may very well have been real but, tragically, misdirected.

p. 101. "Equals at the table"

"[W.E. B.] Du Bois's emphasis was on faith—the belief that the obvious wrongs done to the Black race would be rectified over time and that the Negro, by somehow forging his dual identities into one truly American identity, would at last assume his rightful place at the table of plenty.

At the beginning of this century, Du Bois could not foresee that the shape of the table itself would change, that, perhaps, by the time the Negro found his place at it, the sumptuous meal would have already been devoured; that the souls of Black Folk might be beset with an altogether new crop of hungers grown on the plantations of a sophisticated technology and an accelerating swiftness in the alternating currents of global affairs.

From *The Riot Inside Me: More Trials and Tremors* by Wanda Coleman, p. 56

p. 102. 9/11:

Tim Wise, in his *White Like Me*, discusses this:

"To whites, race war is something *they* do to *us*, that they would initiate, and for no reason, since history has no role to play in the understanding of anything, even the anger about which whites are petrified. It's much like the way whites responded after 9/11, in a way that was nothing if not bizarre to people of color, by saying things like 'Now we know what it's like to be attacked for who we are.' Or '9/11 was the worst act of terrorism in our nation's history.' Or 'Why do they hate us?'

"That most whites would have no idea why these kinds of comments are ludicrous, indeed evidence of an irrationality and disconnect from the real world so profound as to boggle the mind is precisely the point I am trying to make. To white people, at least most whites, we *haven't* been attacked for who we are, and 9/11 *was* the worst act of terrorism, and hating the U.S. makes no sense whatsoever, because in our America, we are the beacons of democratic light in a world of tyranny. That almost no one else experiences the United States in this way escapes us altogether. That lots of nonwhite folks know exactly what it means to be attacked for who they are, what it's like to be terrorized, goes entirely without comment." (p. 58)

p. 102. *Black Like Me*

In 1994, Joshua Solomon, hoping to replicate Griffin's experience, lasted but *two* days as an African American, then wrote about his experience for *The Washington Post*:

"After all of two days, the experiment was over," wrote the young man. "Maybe I was weak, maybe I couldn't hack it. I didn't care. This anger was making me sick and the only antidote I knew was a dose of white skin." (www.mdcbowen.org/p2/rm/white/solomon.html)

p. 103. Tatum, p. 53

p. 103. Father Teeter:

"As the white pastor of a mostly downtown Episcopal con-gregation (the Church of the Good Shepherd), Teeter had made no secret of his racial opinions from the time he arrived in Lynchburg in 1959 … [H]e made a point of not participating in any segregated activities in his new city." (Laurant, p. 118)

p. 106. Dunbar High School's cafeteria

Until the mid-fifties, Dunbar students had *no* cafeteria. Lunches were prepared by the Home Economics students and served on the school's lawn! (*Against All Odds: The Success Story of Dunbar High School* by Delano Douglas for the Lynchburg College Center for the History and Culture of Central Virginia, Dr. Michael Santos, instructor, 2001, p. 7.)

p. 109. MLK HS shooting:

"There's a lack of security, that's the problem with this school," the public high school's student body president, Sabrena Pringle, was quoted as saying after the shooting, despite the fact that Martin Luther King High, like many American high schools these days, has metal detectors at its entrance. Martin Luther King, Jr. would have been seventy-three on the day of the shooting. (www.keystosafersc hools.com/students_concerned21502.htm)

p. 112. Henrico County

Outside of Richmond and pronounced Hen-RYE-co.

p. 114. "I'd shifted locations a little.":

Essayist bell hooks writes: [W]e talk about the way white people who shift locations…begin to see the world differently. Understanding the way racism works [they can see] the way in which whiteness acts to terrorize without seeing [themselves] as bad, or all white people as bad and all black people as good." Quoted in *Beyond the Whiteness of Whiteness: Memoir of a White Mother of Black Sons* by Jane Lazarre, Duke University Press, Durham, 1996, p. 90

✦

A Small Green Island
by Rumi

There is a small green island where one white cow lives
alone, a meadow of an island.

The cow grazes till nightfall, full and fat, but during the
night she panics and grows

thin as a single hair. "What shall I eat tomorrow? There's
nothing left!" By dawn,

the grass has grown up again, waist-high. The cow starts
eating and by dark the

meadow is clipped short. She's full of strength and energy,
but she panics in the dark

as before, and grows abnormally thin overnight. The cow
does this over and over,

and this is all she does. She never thinks, "This meadow has
never failed to grow back.

Why should I be afraid every night that it won't?" The cow
is the bodily soul. The

island field is this world where that grows lean with fear and
fat with blessing, lean

and fat. White cow, don't make yourself miserable with what's
to come, or not to come.

✦

CHAPTER 8
Why should I be afraid every night?

As the conversation between the three of us began to wind down that evening at the Barksdales, I invited Lynda to show me the Lynchburg *she* knew.

Lynda demurred. She had her Randolph-Macon speech to polish, she was tired, she had things to do, she wanted to spend time with her family. Above all, I got the feeling that Lynda Woodruff was wary. Although she'd repeatedly claimed otherwise, a lifetime of hurtful exchanges with White people—including some of the clueless, misinformed things *I'd* said that evening—had left their mark. Given what would ensue, Lynda Woodruff had every reason to be cautious!

The next day, however, Lynda called to say she'd changed her mind. So right after lunch, a light rain falling, I picked her up at her parents' house. The Barksdales' snug, brick ranch is located on a side street of similar neat homes, right off Rivermont Avenue, not far from Randolph-Macon. With her permission, my trusty tape recorder, resting in one of the rental car's cup holders, recorded our conversation. As we pulled away from the curb, Lynda pointed out which neighbors' homes served as her "village."

"That whole thing when Hillary Clinton came out with 'It takes a village...' Well, yeah, but we've known that. Aha! So America acknowledges that...That comes out of African culture. And half the songs, many of the ceremonies, and a lot of our hybrid culture here in the U.S. is anchored in that whole concept of it takes a village.

"When I was growing up, my next-door neighbor—I called her 'Aunt Estelle.' In our back yard was another lady, 'Miss Mabel.' *'Aunt* Mabel.' They both worked with my mother. And if they caught me wrong, they could discipline me, equal to or better than my mom. Then Mom would come home and they'd tell her that they'd had to yank a knot in me or snatch me off the playground or something. And I'd get disciplined again!"

Windshield wipers keeping time, we approached downtown Lynchburg. "Now we're going down Rivermont Avenue passing the mighty Jones Memorial [Library]," commented my tour guide. "And that, to me, was a tower, a symbol of what I couldn't have. The Jones Memorial Library and, believe it or not, the pizza thing on Hollins Mill Road [a teenager hang-out], more than E. C. Glass, to me, those were things that would push my point. Because I needed library access and, of course, it was not available to me. The pizza thing, the Hollins Mill drive-in, was where everybody hung out. It was just a symbol of the social segregation...."

She went on to tell a story of C. G. Harriston, a successful African American businessman she'd known in Danville, who'd bought a custard stand in that city "because he could." Mr. Harriston, like Lynda, like other Virginia African Americans, could remember when they were obliged to buy their hot dogs and ice cream cones "around back by the garbage cans." Mr. Harriston's custard stand was his way of thumbing his nose at those Jim Crow times.

Rivermont Avenue, one of Lynchburg's main thoroughfares, connects the 03 neighborhood with downtown Lynchburg. Closer to downtown, the street descends and the gracious homes lining the broad avenue appear less manicured, more shabby. Crossing the bridge which traverses one of the city's steep ravines, we entered downtown. No longer a vibrant commercial center, downtown Lynchburg nevertheless remains charming for me. I much prefer its steep streets and handsome nineteenth century relics to some sprawling mall. Lynchburg's oldest commercial district is only a few blocks long so we quickly passed through downtown and climbed upward, past an elegant, nineteenth-century residential area, to the site of the former Dunbar High School complex, perched at the top of another Lynchburg hill. I parked the rental in a small parking lot at the end of what appeared to be a horseshoe of buildings.

Lynda explained her former school's layout from the car: "Four buildings, plus Amelia Pride, were in place when I came. This," she said, pointing to a squat, brick building at one end of the horseshoe, "is the boys' mechanical workshop.

Now, remember, for all-Black education, they always had the technical piece along with academic."

My face registered my dismay; I recalled stories from Allison's high school race forum, stories of smart, competent African American students in her Cambridge high school discouraged from taking college-preparatory classes and instead, urged to take shop. Lynda, noting my face, had her own opinion on the subject:

"Realistically, that's okay," she opined. "So the boys' auto workshop, mechanics, carpentry was in that building. Home economics, sewing, cooking, was in the Amelia Pride," she said, pointing to the attractive, one-story cottage at the very top of the horseshoe, named for the founder of both a cooking and a sewing school. "Then the South Building [where the parking lot is now], which is now gone."

"Very compact," I commented, startled. "Very small."

In 1962, when I used to hang out at Hollins Mill drive-in, Dunbar High School and its faceless, nameless students were unseen and unknown, yet loomed large in my imagination. In my mind, *hordes* of Black students attended that other school—over *there*, somewhere.

"The total population of students was like seven hundred rather than the three-thousand [who attended E. C. Glass]."

"And this building," Lynda Woodruff tapped on the window, pointing to a sturdy, three- story brick building, "the middle school building here, now, we had classes in there."

"Do you want to go inside?" I asked her.

"Nah. I have no interest." She'd already told me she didn't want to step foot into E. C. Glass, either. We decided to drive the short distance to the Amelia Pride building but first stopped to explain who we were to two middle-aged White women, crossing guards, I assumed, who were huddled together under an umbrella.

"Hi," Lynda said to them, rolling down her rain-speckled window. "Just an alum from many years ago."

"Hi, how you doing?" they replied as if they knew her.

"I'm Lynda Woodruff. Thank you for letting us park without thinking we were going to do something foul and ridiculous. I—we should have acknowledged that at the beginning, given just what happened on Monday [the shooting at Martin Luther King, Jr. High School]."

We chitchatted with the two women who assured us they'd thought we were there simply to pick up a child. What, I wondered, did they imagine the relationship to be between Lynda and me? Their cordial greeting to this attractive African American woman beside me confused me, yet another reminder that I'd not understood White culture in the segregated South when I lived in Lynchburg and had no more clarity, forty years later, about how Whites would interpret the two of us sitting in a rental car. Nor how they viewed this dangerous-feeling world.

After a close look at the Amelia Pride cottage, Lynda and I pulled away from the parking lot to take a look at Dunbar's athletic fields, located behind her former school and further down the steep hill. "That's Diamond Hill Church [Virgil Wood's church]," she pointed to a spired, brick church at the bottom of an angular ravine, just past the athletic fields, maybe three blocks below us. "We could walk to [civil rights] mass meetings. See how close it is?"

To see how close Virgil Wood's church and the city's African American high school were, I saw not only the proximity of those two buildings, I understood something:

I saw how the African American community's churches, "spring[s] of cool water in a weary land," were linked to the spiritually-based nonviolent movement and to a generation of eager, bright, idealistic students—and regular churchgoers—like Lynda Woodruff and Owen Cardwell. And I saw, because I'd never set foot in Dunbar's neighborhood until that afternoon, how I hadn't understood this basic, fundamental linkage.

"See?! See?!" I hear myself shout on the tape as I, literally, see this linkage and also realize that this basic understanding has been made possible only because Lynda guided me here. Suddenly I saw the civil rights pioneer sitting beside me drinking deeply from the Diamond Hill spring.

Leaving the Dunbar neighborhood, we tried to make our way towards the Legacy Museum of African American History on Monroe Street but somehow kept ending up on streets named for other American presidents, streets like Polk or Tyler, instead. "Don't you know your presidents in order?" Lynda teased.

And, again, I experienced a little frisson. This almost-stranger beside me went to the same high school I did, took classes with the same teachers, and was expected to learn the same body of perhaps useless and certainly arbitrary information—our presidents in order, for example. Lynda Darnell Woodruff and Patricia Amey Wild will therefore be forever connected by the same tests and quizzes and term papers which gauged how well both of us had absorbed the same facts and opinions and half-truths *someone* thought we both should know.

Focused on finding Monroe Street, I nevertheless caught brief glimpses of imposing, expensively restored Victorians next to boarded-up, neglected homes in the neighborhood we were driving through. These historic homes reminded me of a brief exchange with Georgia Barksdale the night before. She and Ed on their way to a meeting on historic districts, Georgia had paused at the family room's back door: "If you lived here, would you like the historic [districts]?"

"Yeah," I responded almost automatically: Aesthetics, architectural integrity, preservation; isn't that what historic districts mean? Of course I support that. As a matter of fact, at one point in my life I'd even owned a home in a historic district.

"Well," Georgia Barksdale replied sweetly, "my husband is against you."

Seeing Lynchburg's gentrification for the first time with Lynda, I understood why the former city councilman would side with those less-affluent people who could no longer afford to live in an "up and coming neighborhood."

Embarrassed by my insensitivity, I asked Lynda a question I'd meant to ask the night before: "Separate but equal—did you have new textbooks?"

"We had new textbooks but probably half of what we needed. The library, I will never forget as long as I live... When I was there in 1960...the encyclopedia was a 1947 Funk and Wagnalls.

"But the teachers were extraordinary. The Black teachers were way more credentialed than the White teachers that we met at Glass but way underexposed....We had no chemistry equipment and the most brilliant Chemistry teacher in the world, Mr. W. E. Clark. He may well be there tonight, as well [at Randolph-Macon]. One of the most incredible minds, definitively a genius, again, and nothing to teach with. So totally, totally, totally creative."

As she was saying this, we arrived at the Legacy Museum where, five months later, I would meet Mr. W. E. Clark.

The Legacy Museum was closed; getting back in the car, I told Lynda of visiting the museum the day after the Restoration Jubilee conference. I'd mentioned Jerry Falwell's participation at the conference with one of the museum's curators, an elderly African American man, dressed in a suit and tie.

"Tell me," the elderly gentleman had asked, "Did Jerry Falwell apologize?"

The Legacy Museum is located on the crest of a steep hill. We now drove down that hill's other side, past Pierce Street, where Anne Spencer and Whirlwind Johnson once lived. The topography less dramatic on the other side, we drove through a residential area of more modest, post-war homes, towards the new Jones Memorial Library and its Dr. Martin Luther King, Jr. Center for Human Rights. On the way, Dr. Woodruff shared another story.

"They published in the paper that my IQ was 88! I have tons of tee shirts that say '88.' I have one that says '88' on the front, and 'Read my résumé' on the back! So obviously, that was an ego-defense mechanism on my part. Even though I laugh about it."

When our sprawling alma mater came into view, Dr. Woodruff changed her mind: "Let's go in," she said. "So we can give our salute! We might have to have a passport to get on campus!" she added nervously.

That same evening, during her keynote address at Randolph-Macon, Lynda Woodruff would talk about our visit to E. C. Glass.

"We walked the [same] halls," she told the chapel audience, "that [Owen and I] walked on January 29, 1962. It was a spooky, eerie, interesting, warm, fuzzy, prickly kind of a feeling."

That it was. Past three o'clock, the school was as deserted as downtown Lynchburg. On our way to the cafeteria where Thelma Campbell had befriended a silently weeping teenaged girl, we met a couple of African American students. "Where are you going to college?" Dr. Woodruff asked them after we'd introduced ourselves. The young people shrugged.

"No," she tried again. "I'm asking you where you're planning to go to college?" They mumbled something about lack of funds.

"You do not understand," she said, handing each of them one of her cards, embossed with her name and North Georgia College and State University. "I said *where* are you planning to go?" The two Glass students smiled as they pocketed her card; now they understood: Lynda was offering to help them with their college application process.

Down the hall from the cafeteria, Lynda pointed out her locker; I marveled that she still remembered the number. We then entered her and Owen's homeroom, where I had once studied Virginia and American History and where, as she told the Randolph-Macon audience that evening, she'd remembered a Confederate flag on display.

"Owen will be pleased to know that when we entered that classroom today, in the year 2002, forty years later, the Confederate flag is gone."

The classroom was still arranged exactly as it had been two-score years ago—in rows. On the walls, however, were pictures of Malcolm X, Martin Luther King; there were even pictures of Owen Cardwell and Lynda Woodruff on display. Correcting papers at one of the desks was the classroom's pretty, White English teacher, Ms. Sherry Scruggs. Lynda, after examining the classroom's walls, walked over to where Ms. Scruggs was working: "Why the diversity?" she asked.

Seemingly not flustered by Dr. Woodruff's brusque question, Ms. Scruggs began to explain that as a younger woman, she'd considered Malcolm X to be "the devil, but that"—Lynda interrupted her.

Without thinking, I nudged my companion. "Shh," I told her. "She's telling us her conversion story. Don't interrupt!" then panicked when I remembered that I'd once promised myself *never* to tell Lynda Woodruff what to do.

But Lynda Woodruff immediately and graciously apologized; Ms. Scruggs then told of reading Malcolm X's diary—which she now assigns to her students—and how she'd come to view the Black Power leader differently.

We thanked Ms. Scruggs for her time, then continued our stroll. Needing to use a bathroom, we ducked into one of the high school's restrooms, less brightly lit than I remembered but clean and relatively graffiti-free.

Was this it? I wondered as Lynda and I closed the doors to our respective toilet stalls. Was this the moment my leading was supposed to be about? That the two of us, who'd once used segregated restrooms and attended segregated schools, shared a restroom at E. C. Glass without comment?

"You know," I said as we walked toward the high school's two cafeterias, "Miss Hight, my chemistry teacher, told us one day that the reason General Electric had moved all of us to Lynchburg was because they'd sent representatives to E. C. Glass and that these GE people had been impressed by the cleanliness of Glass's restrooms. Can you imagine?" I asked her, my voice rising, "My family had to move to this stupid town—" Lynda winced; Lynchburg was, after all, her hometown—"because of *bathrooms*?

"I know that story is nothing compared to what you and Owen had to go through," I added lamely.

"That's all right," she said, as we walked down the locker-lined hallway. "I just wish I'd known that White students were going through things like that."

Lynda and I cried as we stood in the doorway of the cafeteria where she'd first met her "survival rope." And I silently thanked Spirit for all the Thelma Campbells of Lynchburg's civil rights movement who, without fanfare, had offered strength and support to pioneers like Lynda and Owen. And I thanked God for this precious experience, this amazing afternoon with Lynda Woodruff, which I, "lean with fear," had doubted would ever happen.

✦

During that January 2002 trip to Lynchburg, I stayed at a charming, Victorian bed and breakfast; let's call this B&B the "Cavalier."

After a couple of disquieting conversations with the Cavalier's owners my first day there, I'd gone to bed uneasy to be sleeping across the hall from two people whose right-wing, NRA-supportive views differed so dramatically from my own. My Flight or Fight instinct triggered, I tossed and turned in my bed most of the night. Traffic sounds on a busy Lynchburg street died down, the comings and goings of city buses—there seemed to be a bus stop right under my window—ended, but in the early hours of January 16, 2002, the day after Martin Luther King, Jr.'s birthday, I was still awake, still wondering if I should have braced a chair under my room's doorknob, then scolding myself for being such an idiot.

When insomnia strikes, I try giving myself some sort of mental assignment: how to write that all-important first sentence for an upcoming *Somerville Journal* column, for example, which sometimes allows me to sleep. So, wide awake in Lynchburg, Virginia, I mulled what to read at an upcoming poetry reading in Somerville, scheduled for the Martin Luther King, Jr. holiday the following Monday. "Come hear some of the poems that your friends and neighbors have turned to for meaning, solace, and perspective in the weeks since September 11th," read the reading flier. What poem should I read, I wondered.

It was almost dawn when suddenly I heard something I recognized immediately: A deep rumbling from the B&B's basement followed by the cheerful sound of clanging radiators as the heat comes on in an old Victorian house. The radiators in my Victorian home make exactly the same noises. And I remembered Robert Hayden's poem, "Those Winter

Sundays" and how, two or three years before, when teaching poetry to a class of adult learners, Hayden's poem had stopped the loud complaints of "Why do we have to read this stuff?" Those GED students, men and women who'd dropped out of school years ago, whose experiences of poetry, literature, art, indeed learning, itself, had been tainted by shoddy teaching and the trauma of their own lives, had been deeply moved by Hayden's words.

Surely, I thought, early-morning light just beginning to brighten my room's shades, the stuff of good poetry is in this house. Universal truths are at work and at play here, too. Surely, I thought, remembering those initially balky adult learners, transcendence happens. I've been too caught up in my own quest, too focused on my considerable limitations, too aware of my own White privilege, too judgmental of other White people to acknowledge such a possibility.

The Cavalier's hostess showed me the way. My last morning in Lynchburg, I was having breakfast alone, seated at one end of the dining room table, fresh flowers before me, a harp CD playing, when the B&B's owner stepped out of the kitchen.

"We were opposed to integration," she said after we'd chatted about why I had come to Lynchburg. She told me about growing up in a state in the deep South, she talked about making a career choice based on wanting to avoid African Americans: "I didn't think any of *them* would ever…" She talked about the integration of schools and public swimming pools. This led to a question of where I'd swum when I lived in Lynchburg.

My family had belonged to the Boonsboro Country Club, I explained. "Oh, then," she said, smiling. "Then you were safe." She's afraid of The Other, I realized. Wouldn't she be shocked to learn that for me, *she* is an Other! Aloud, I repeated her word to affirm for myself my connection with her fear: "Yes," I said slowly, remembering my impulse to brace my bedroom door two nights before, "I was 'safe.'"

Racists are afraid? They're not simply evil, hateful people? I mulled that over as I began the plane journey from Lynchburg to Boston—via Charlotte.

And a buried memory surfaced: The night I sat in "the Colored Section" to see "Porgy and Bess" at a downtown Lynchburg movie theater that Owen Cardwell would eventually desegregate.

I don't remember who my date had been that night in 1960. I do know this young man and I had underestimated the movie's popularity and had arrived at the box office too late to be able to sit downstairs. I remember my keen disappointment; I had been waiting to see this movie for months. (Movies took their time getting to Lynchburg.) "There are seats in the Colored Section," the ticket seller—now merely a remembered voice—noted reluctantly. "What do you want to do?" my date asked me.

Had that young man been merely chivalrous? Had he been automatically acting on his "white southern tribal values," to always politely ask the young lady's preference? Or was he tacitly acknowledging my Yankee background and therefore the possibility that I might be more willing to sit in the balcony of a segregated movie theater than one of his Lynchburg-born dates? I shall never know.

I can see myself on the sidewalk in front of a brightly lit downtown movie theater. I remember the ticket-seller's and my date's fear. When my escort and I climbed the carpeted stairs to the balcony, I brought their fear with me. Did those two southerners understand something I didn't? Would we be attacked? Did my determination to see a long-anticipated movie put two White teenagers in danger? Suddenly afraid, the lights already dimmed, I searched for two vacant seats amongst the rows of darkened faces.

That crowded and capacious balcony contained more African Americans in one place than I had ever before experienced. But here is what I remember: How quiet that crowd had been; I remember no hoots, no catcalls, no comments. And I remember this: How quickly, in those first seconds in the weirdly quiet balcony, as Gershwin's overture played and the opening credits rolled, how my fear gave way to a recognition of the *resignation* among those seated men and women. "They won't hurt me," I told myself. "They've seen two terrified-looking White kids stumble into Colored Sections before. They won't hurt me. Jim Crow has worn them out."

Observing the long security lines at the Charlotte airport, the B&B owner's words kept coming back to me, underlined by the Fear-of-Other, Post-September 11 world I witnessed all around me. Raised in the segregated South, no doubt told chilling, horrific stories, denied any opportunity to ever "connect with the feeling of kind heart" of any person of color, denied, perhaps to have the kind of special, woman-to-woman conversation I'd so relished with Sharon Boswell (which, of course, until very late in my life, I, myself had been denied!), of *course* the Cavalier owner was afraid!

Flying over my country at thirty-five thousand feet, I continued to connect with that B&B owner's fear. Fear of Other? Just a few months before, like many Americans, I had been so terrified to step outside my house that I'd spent three days in my darkened bedroom watching a jumbo jet smash into the World Trade tower again and again on TV. Fear of Other? I'd tossed and turned in a Victorian-style brass bed because I'd found a southern couple's political views so disquieting. I could connect with that woman's fear, I could even have compassion for her fear, I realized, without having to connect with, or pass judgment on, or to condone her racism. "Out beyond ideas of wrongdoing and right-doing/there is a field,/I'll meet you there," Rumi says. In my heart, I could meet the B&B owner in that wide meadow of fear and vulnerability.

And, I reminded myself as the plane approached Boston Harbor, a meadow which "has never failed to grow back." For I recalled a conversation I'd had with Alex Kern, a younger member of my Quaker meeting, in the fall of 2000. Alex, too, had applied for a Special Sources Fund grant from Friends Meeting at Cambridge. While discussing our respective applications, Alex had offered some very useful and insightful advice, advice which would greatly strengthen my application.

"But, Alex," I pointed out. "You and I are in competition for this grant. Why are you telling me this?"

Young enough to be my son, Alex nevertheless gave me a patient, loving smile worthy of a wizened saint: "Patricia," he said gently. "You must be a subscriber to the theory that there isn't enough. But there is. The Universe has enough for both of us."

NOTES: "Why Should I be Afraid Every Night?"

p. 124. "spring[s] of cool water in a weary land": "Whether in 'shouting ecstasy' or in quiet faith, whether whipped by a preacher into emotional frenzy or led to the good life by words and deeds, whether in a fine church on an elm-shaded avenue or in the alley shack that once housed a blacksmith shop, Virginia Negroes still look upon religion as supplying a great need, as a spring of cool water in a weary land." (*Negro in Virginia*, p. 289)

p. 125. Historic District
From 1976 until 1979, I lived in Wethersfield, Connecticut's historic district although not in one of the district's carefully restored eighteenth-century homes.

p.130. "Safe"
The B&B owner unwittingly repeated the same word used by Virginia legislator Henry Berry in 1831: "If we could extinguish the capacity to see the light, our work would be completed; [slaves] would then be on a level with the beasts of the field and we should be safe."

p. 131. "White tribal values."
Rebecca Owen as quoted in *Journeys That Opened Up the World: Women, Student Christian Movements, and Social Justice, 1955 - 1975*, edited by Sara M. Evans, Rutgers University Press, New Brunswick, NJ, 2003, p. 69

p. 132. "Connect with the feeling of kind heart."
The Places that Scare You: A Guide to Fearlessness in Difficult Times, by (American-Buddhist nun) Pema Chodron, Shambhala Publications, Inc., Boston, MA, 2001, p. 46.

✦

Epitome
by Anne Spencer

Once the world was young
For I was twenty and very old
And you and I knew all the answers
What the day was, how the hours would turn
One dial was there to see
Now the world is old and I am still young
For the young know nothing, nothing.

✦

CHAPTER 9
Still young

In early 2004, with much trepidation—I had no idea how justified!—I mailed Lynda and Owen a first draft of our book, entitled *Deep River*. Because I believed that this leading had been about that wonderful afternoon Lynda and I shared, I had structured *Deep River* so that it culminated with that extraordinary afternoon. Lynda's guided tour through Lynchburg, our walk together through the halls of E. C. Glass, the transformation of a public high school classroom, where a Confederate flag once hung, to a warm and inviting space where Lynda's and Owen's and Malcolm X's photographs were prominently displayed; surely this leading was about that experience!

To build the drama, I had emphasized in that draft my initial reaction to Lynda leaving her seven-pound appointment book back at her office. Naively, I believed that she, like other readers, would appreciate the gradually unfolding story of our friendship. But Lynda did not see it that way. Deeply hurt, she arranged a three-way conference call; listening to her angrily read passages she had found painful, I felt physically ill.

Owen had his issues with that first draft as well: *His* sense of how the Randolph-Macon audience had reacted to his anti-abortion statements had been completely different from mine, for example. In his usual calm and quiet tone, Owen offered his theory as to why his and my readings of that audience had so vastly differed.

"I believe that my views are closer to Jerry Falwell's than to yours," the Baptist preacher explained.

"Now that's just sad," Lynda chimed in, a brief and welcomed moment of unanimity.

The three-way conversation continued but after awhile, Owen bowed out: "This is between you two, I'm going to hang up," he announced wearily.

Lynda and I continued "dialoging," as Owen would say. She told me some other things wrong with the manuscript. Because I'd not yet located O. C. Cardwell's manuscript, I did not understand, for example, how divided Lynchburg's African American community had been by Lynda's, Owen's, Brenda Hughes's, and Cecelia Jackson's transfer requests. Although I had understood how pivotal Dunbar High School had been to the Black community, I had failed to grasp that for some members of the city's Black community, particularly for Dunbar's teachers and staff, those four transfer requests might pose a threat, a potential beginning of the end for Dunbar, the African American community's "social center, the information center, the meeting place, the home away from home."

Had I considered Dunbar High School's role in Lynchburg more deeply, I would have realized that, indeed, Dunbar teachers and staff had every right to feel threatened. Just as the Black school's personnel had feared, Lynchburg's desegregation process ultimately resulted in Dunbar High School being closed. From my reading, I knew that this pattern of Black schools being abandoned after school desegregation had been repeated throughout the South. Tragically, in Lynchburg's case, Dunbar High School, this all-important institution for the African American community, was razed, as well.

By the end of the conversation, although still hurt, still angry, Lynda Woodruff, to my amazement, declared herself my friend and willing to keep talking. Praise Spirit!

Deeply ashamed, I sought help from Friends Meeting. And found it. Wendy Sanford and Susan Lloyd McGarry, two gifted writers I now met with regularly, gently acknowledged my shame and held me in prayer. Patricia Watson, former editor of *Peacework* magazine and a foremost leader of Friends for Racial Justice (FORJ), the anti-racism committee at Friends Meeting, graciously agreed to read the offending manuscript, editing pencil in hand, and to patiently sit with me for hours as we worked our way through *Deep River* page by page.

As the days after that three-way telephone conference increased, I panicked. Was this how this leading was to end?

In *White Like Me,* Tim Wise writes:

And although we have to forgive ourselves for the mistakes we make, we must first acknowledge them. We must face up to the fact that in our resistance [to racism and White privilege], we too often reinforce all the hierarchical nonsense we swear we oppose, much of it racist at its core. Only by being called out, as I was, can we learn this in most cases. Only by being exposed to our flaws, forced to deal with them, and to learn from them, can we move forward, can we strengthen our resistance in the future.

On Sunday-morning meetings for worship, in deep, nourishing meetings with Susan Lloyd and Wendy, on long, meditative walks, and in my journal I asked Spirit: Had my own racism been the root of my naive decision to write that first draft the way I had?

Over time, I realized I had written about Lynda and Owen as if they were historical figures, abstractions, fictitious characters in a piece of writing I'd crafted so as to tell a compelling story. As if the three of us had never met, as if we had never broken bread nor worshipped nor laughed together. As if I had not sat in the Barksdales' family room listening to Owen and Lynda's painful stories. Why had I imagined that someone who *told* me she is called Nigger every day of her life would appreciate my literary approach? Why had I imagined that my own political and religious views would not color how I interpreted what I saw and heard during Owen's Randolph-Macon speech? Why, indeed.

When Lynda finally e-mailed me in early April, just to say hello, after several weeks of chilling silence, I was euphoric. Her brief but warm communication seemed to mean that she was giving me another chance to redeem myself. That evening, however, at a chamber music concert, I panicked: "What *should* have struck me before this hit me hard: What if I mess up again?" I wrote later that night in my journal. "What if this is too hard? What if I'm not good enough? Certainly these non-writing days [I had stopped writing until what should happen next became clear] make such realistic questions much more accessible, somehow. So. This leading is about humility as well as about a clueless White woman learning about two extraordinary people."

During this period of reflection and discernment, I attended a three-hour conference at the Harvard School of Education in honor of the fiftieth anniversary of *Brown versus Board of Education*. Several of the school's graduate students presented research which clearly demonstrated, fifty years after the Supreme Court had declared segregated schools to be unconstitutional, that students who attended public schools in the greater-Boston area were still very much separated by race. For many of the African Americans who attended this all-too-brief conference, however, the event was not so much about the dissemination of depressing research—research they undoubtedly already knew. For them, the conference offered an opportunity to tell their stories of racism, of Jim Crow schools, and their experiences during the civil rights movement.

As I walked home from this curtailed conference, I reflected on the PowerPoint presentations I'd seen, the grad students' neat charts and tidy graphs which outlined not only greater-Boston segregation patterns but also how poorly inner-city students scored on the Massachusetts achievement tests known as the Massachusetts Comprehensive Assessment System (the MCAS, pronounced "EM-cas."). Had those young people been surprised that for so many African American attendees, the need to "testify" had been so much more compelling than a close analysis of test scores? And with great sadness I remembered my initial commitment, in the earliest days of this leading, to "*use* my Whiteness to tell [African American] stories." How little I had understood how much my Whiteness was going to get in my way.

I came home to discover an e-mail from Lynda inviting me to a Lynchburg *Brown* celebration in two weeks!

✦

On my flight to Lynchburg for the *Brown* celebration, I read and reread photocopied documents, copies of the actual 1961 Lynchburg school desegregation court decisions and transcripts of the Lynchburg School Board minutes from 1961 and 1962, which Lynda had recently sent me. During our bumpy conference call, Dr. Lynda Woodruff—who had successfully completed her doctoral dissertation and therefore knew far more than I about research—let me know that in addition to my lack of understanding about the complex Dunbar High School situation, my research concerning the actual court cases and the Lynchburg School Board actions from that time had been inadequate. So on her own, Lynda had hired her friend, Marian Anderson Jones, to track down much-needed documents which she then mailed to me.

How to convey my feelings on that flight? To say I was enormously, tearfully grateful to attend this celebration is only a small part of it. Humbled? Absolutely. Chastened? You bet. Terrified to mess up again? Ditto. The word that best describes what I felt as I watched the rolling hills of Central Virginia undulate below, however, is "touched." Despite my obvious shortcomings, Owen Cardwell and Lynda Woodruff had decided to trust me enough to give me another chance. To invite me to Lynchburg was to hand me a precious, deeply moving gift to treasure and to treat tenderly. To honor Owen and Lynda's trust seemed as insistent a commandment as any nudge or prompting from Spirit.

Lynda picked me up at the airport. Before delivering me to my hotel downtown— which she had generously arranged to pay for—we stopped at a mall near the airport to buy shoes for the celebration that night. Like that back seat conversation with Sharon Boswell when she and I had discussed where we had bought our dresses for Owen's anniversary banquet, I so appreciated this shopping expedition. To fuss over just the right shade of beige pumps offered Lynda and me a wonderful opportunity to simply be together again.

Lynda came up the elevator with me to my spacious hotel room. The fourth-floor view offered a glimpse of two sites enormously significant during my adolescence: General Electric's downtown offices were in the foreground and a few streets away could be seen the YMCA where I'd once read *Jesus the Carpenter's Son* in my Unitarian Sunday school classes.

Because of our warm, woman-to-woman shopping expedition, I did not see myself as Lynda's interviewer and therefore did not turn on my tape recorder as she and I chatted, nor, unfortunately, did I save the piece of paper upon which Lynda diagrammed the complexity of her professional life. Had she not been forced to interrupt this illustrated explanation so she could go home to bathe and dress for the upcoming ceremony, that piece of paper would have been even more covered with notations and the initials of numerous professional organizations.

After she had left, I strolled through downtown, the May sun hot against my skin. After a brief stop at Bowen's Jewelry Store on Main Street to say hello to Jane Barringer Bowen, my senior-year English teacher (who, ever-gracious, pretended to remember me), I thought about what Lynda had just shared about her complicated life: Lynda's former students, "Woody's Babies," as they're called, keep in close touch with their beloved teacher. Woody's Babies—who even have their own tee shirts—recently started a physical therapy school in Utah; Lynda's credit card underwrote this project. I thought about the first time Lynda Woodruff and I met. And in a moment not unlike when I understood the relationship between Diamond Hill Baptist Church and Dunbar High School, I began to let the heaviness of Dr. Lynda Woodruff's seven-pound appointment book sink down to that seed God planted in my heart.

✦

An integrated E. C. Glass jazz band performed "Take the A Train" as celebrants for Lynchburg's 50th anniversary of *Brown versus The Board of Education* gathered in the high school's commodious, sky-blue lobby. Above the lobby hung a blue-and-white banner which proclaimed E. C. Glass to be "A Nationally Recognized School of Excellence." The well-dressed crowd, largely African American, had come to witness the installation of a "portrait," which featured photographs of Lynda, Owen, and Carl Hutcherson, Sr., Lynchburg's first African American School Board member. Crystabel Harris, the former Dunbar student who had tried unsuccessfully to transfer to Glass, was among the sixty or so people there. So were members of Owen's and Lynda's families, Darrell Laurant, and retired Dunbar High School teacher, W. E. Clark.

I do not know which was more shocking: That the program began with an African American student reading Anne Spencer's "White Things," a diatribe against lynching and perhaps the Lynchburg poet's most angry poem? Or that no one in the crowd reacted to "They pyred a race of black, black men,/And burned them to ashes white, then,/Laughing, a young man claimed a skull, For the skull of a black is white, not dull./"?

After Carl Hutcherson, Jr., Lynchburg's mayor in 2004, gave a tearful tribute to his father, Lynda and Owen spoke. Unnerved by the predominantly African American crowd— "It didn't feel right," she would explain the next day—the usual charismatic Lynda Woodruff did not connect with the crowd quite as effectively as she had at Owen's banquet or at Randolph-Macon. Owen used the short period of time allotted to him to bemoan how much of his time he spent these days "trying to keep young Black men out of jail."

But if the Celebrating Our History venue had felt awkward for the pair, speaking before racially mixed Glass classes the next day was clearly the opposite. From the moment principal Susan Morrison explained who Lynda and Owen were and, spontaneously, fifty or so students gave the firsts a standing ovation, Lynda and Owen were in their element. Charming, moving, the pair told their stories: "This is not ancient history, this is American history," Owen joked. "It was *our* decision [to cross that threshold]," Lynda emphasized.

The pioneers offered their perspective on desegregation: "Look to your right, look to your left," Lynda suggested. Students could expect to work with people that looked like Glass students. So that not only were her listeners receiving an excellent education—"I am so proud of the education I got at E. C. Glass," she declared—they were being prepared for a racially-mixed, diverse future.

Lynda and Owen gave their talk in the school's double-sized band room; they leaned against the band room stage as they talked. Listening to them, I recalled that freshman band yearbook photograph of Owen Cardwell with his trombone, "one skinny, frightened black kid tucked away in a corner somewhere." On May 18, 2004, a "Casual Day" at E. C. Glass, Dr. Owen C. Cardwell was no longer tucked in the band room's corner but alongside his good friend Dr. Lynda Woodruff, a featured speaker at the front of the room.

After their highly successful presentations at Glass, Lynda, Owen, and I drove back to my hotel and, over lunch, discussed the offending first draft and what we hoped for next. Mindful of Lynda's brief explanation the day before of just *some* of her professorial obligations and wanting to make the best use of our time together, I asked Owen if he would mind sending me a copy of his résumé. "I know nothing about your professional life after E. C. Glass," I explained. "Your tenure at Concord Church [in Boston], for example."

"He spent the next four-five-six years driving me nuts, in Vietnam, without communicating. As if I didn't care what was going on," Lynda remembered.

"I was in the Vietnam War, but I was in Korea," Owen reminded his friend. "Something hit me when you asked me that," Owen said over his salad. "I had to send a copy of my résumé back to a former church. I was told that somebody remarked: 'He didn't need to send a three-page résumé! He didn't need to send all that!'

"Hey! That's my résumé. My résumé is my résumé."

"If they reacted to three pages, I have a problem!" Lynda exclaimed.

"It's the truth for both of you," I acknowledged, Lynda's diagram explaining her professional life fresh in my mind, "that because of your experiences and who you were, people counted on you so much and you were asked to do so much."

I was referring to the pair's professional lives; Lynda, however, connected my statement to her ground-breaking high school experience.

"And we did not have the privilege of failing," Lynda added. "Can you just even imagine what would have happened if any one of the four of us [Owen, Lynda, Brenda Hughes, and Cecelia Jackson] had not walked across that stage on June 12, 1965?"

"A very seemingly innocent statement: 'You're a credit to your race.' People don't realize the enormous burden that is placed on someone—anyone—but especially a teenager," Owen noted. "My whole race is being judged by my success or failure. That's too much of a burden for anybody."

"If I'm wrong, tell me, but I don't think they do that to White people," Lynda commented.

"What do the two of you do with that sense of burden and responsibility for your entire race?" I asked them both later.

"I got tired," Lynda replied. "I got tired. I don't mind knowing things. I don't mind sharing things. But I won't accept the burden of the race."

Owen responded to my question: "I think that, from a historical, cultural vantage point, there's a process for African Americans and it's been called a lot of different things—the pop term, now, is generativity—the passing on of what I know, what I've experienced to my sphere of influence.

"Can't do it for everybody. I'm not the Great White Hope—" [He corrected himself as Lynda teased "See? I told you he thought he was White!"]—"Great Hope for the Black Race.

"I think last year [when he had experienced serious health problems] I kind of came to grips with that. Like Lynda, I had reached certain heights...At forty-four, I was heading up a state agency under the [Virginia Governor L. Douglas] Wilder administration, another first.

"In my pastoral career, I had been at Concord Baptist Church and now, here I am, with a church that is ten years old that I organized. [I was] preaching to a congregation that had a thousand folks in attendance on Sunday and now [I'm preaching] to a congregation that barely has sixty adults on Sunday. Yet I feel more successful now.

"That's why, doing today [at E. C. Glass] was much more important to me than last night. Because maybe somebody heard," Owen concluded.

"You know what I saw," Lynda began, "sitting up there, yesterday? And I don't know how I feel because I haven't had time to process, yet...While I am extremely grateful, the audience symbolized to me everything that is wrong: it was segregated. White administration, Black audience. It didn't feel good. And I love everybody sitting in that room!"

"My grandson came to me last night," Owen related, "the one that kept wanting to get in the pictures. He said, 'Grandpa, I want to show you something.' So he took me over to one of the showcases, and I don't know if you paid any attention to them but one of them had a cast head of a man with a cigar in his mouth. He pointed to it and he said, 'What's that?'

"I said, 'I don't know.'

"I wonder what they're going to do with those portraits? Will they just hang there? Or is there a real purpose for them? I saw L. H. McQue's [Glass's principal when Lynda and Owen were there] picture, there in the hall. And I bet you that there were a dozen people in that audience, if that many, who even knew who he was. And probably two out of that dozen cared.

"I don't want our picture to be just another picture hanging. The kids who were in those two sessions [today] got something. What about the rest of the school?"

✦

Slowly sipping a frothy chai, I sit at a small, round, black, slightly gummy table at the Diesel Café and, using a Pilot pen and lined paper, write. Other writers, one per table, sit nearby; furrow-browed, they stare at their laptop screens as their fingers nimbly dance over their keyboards. My favorite café in Somerville's hip Davis Square, the Diesel is independently owned and therefore a favorite hangout for anyone eschewing Starbucks; Diesel is also a popular gathering place for greater-Boston gays, lesbians, bi's and transgendered folks.

Like many cafés, Diesel exhibits an ever-changing array of local artists' work. The current exhibit, which I am too busy writing to view, combines black-and-white drawings displayed beside written narratives. A young man in his late teens, his abundant, curly hair a nimbus around his head and dressed in tee shirt, shorts, and Tevas, slowly walks from drawing to drawing. He's reading every word, every single word, I realize. The young man's intensity pulls me from my work.

Pay attention, my Inner Voice whispers. There's something here for you to learn.

And it is this: Every young person experiences stories, history, parables, and fables as if they are the first person to learn these things. No matter how ancient the tale, if heard by young ears, it is as if the story is happening for the very first time. And no matter how many of the previous generations may know the narrative by heart, for a young man or woman, it is a just-written story, displayed on a café wall, perhaps, to stumble upon and to savor.

✦

Lynchburg's Warwick Press mails me its latest publication, a thick, amply illustrated book by James M. Elson entitled *Lynchburg, Virginia: The First Two Hundred Years, 1786–1986*. After spending several days reading Dr. Elson's carefully researched, impressive work, I place his book on a shelf in my study next to Darrell Laurant's *A City Unto Itself: Lynchburg, Virginia in the 20th Century* and Benjamin Muses's *Virginia's Massive Resistance*.

Does the Universe need yet another book on Lynchburg history or the desegregation of one of Virginia's public schools, I wonder?

p. 136. "social center, the information center," etc.

W. E. Clark said this in a November 16, 2003, letter to me. A former Dunbar High School science teacher, now retired, I happened to meet him on the steps of the Legacy Museum in June of 2002. His complete statement re Dunbar was:

"It was clear to see that nearly everything related to life in the Black community either flowed into or out from Dunbar. Dunbar was for the Black citizens the social center, the information center, the meeting place, the home away from home, and the safe haven for all life."

p. 139. Marian Anderson Jones:

At that time, Ms. Jones was the deputy assistant to former Ambassador Andrew Young.

p. 140. Dr. Lynda Woodruff's stellar career:

In 2006, Lynda retired but, not surprisingly, is still actively involved in a number of projects.

p. 141. Crystabel Harris:

From "No Matter How Long: The Struggle to Integrate the Public Schools in Lynchburg, Virginia, 1954–1970," by Henry Faulkner Heil, University of South Carolina–Dept. of History, 2001, p. 30:

In 1959, Crystabel Harris requested a transfer from Dunbar High School to E. C. Glass. Crystabel Harris was the daughter of Fred Harris, a Lynchburg insurance salesman and bail bondsman for Lynchburg civil rights activists. Fred Harris's employer, a White-owned insurance firm, threatened to revoke his license if his daughter's case drew too much "negative" attention. The Harris family tried, unsuccessfully, to enlist other Dunbar students to challenge Lynchburg's segregated schools.

Miss Harris's transfer request was sent by the Lynchburg School Board—without its signature of approval—to the Pupil Placement Board (PPB) in Richmond. The PPB realized Miss Harris was African American because the Lynchburg School Board had not signed its approval. The PPB denied her request on the basis that she lived closer to Dunbar than to Glass. Lynchburg's School

Board, therefore, could claim the decision to deny Miss Harris's request was out of its hands.

Discouraged by the lack of community support, the Harris family discontinued seeking a transfer.

✦

Empire
by Susan Lloyd McGarry

Guaman Poma, native to the Andes,
wrote to the King of Spain in 1615:
If you knew
what they are doing
in your name, you would cry
such tears, enough tears
to cleanse the world,
to start again.
The King did not reply.

Brothers and sisters,
friends and children, neighbors:
if you only knew
what is being
done in our name,
the suffering, the hunger—
but you do know and so do I.
But we don't know
how to stop. And now
there's more talk of war.

Maybe if we really heard
the stories, let them
into our bodies,
we could let our tears
fall and fall, we
could be clean,
there might be a way
to start again.

✦

Reprinted by permission.

CHAPTER 10
In Our Name

My fifth trip to Lynchburg had been scheduled around my expectation that by late September the 2004 hurricane season would be over. But as I flew south on September 27, powerful winds from Hurricane Jeanne moved north; the rough flight announced that bad weather lay ahead. Am I crazy? Have I lost my mind? I wondered, as dark, ominous clouds whipped past my window and the plane heaved and rocked.

Heavy rains began just after I landed. Nervous about driving in the rain at night, I called Ed and Georgia Barksdale, who were to be interviewed that evening, to ask if we could meet during the daylight instead. Although busy people, they graciously acceded to my request.

The interview began with Georgia relating her earliest "separate but equal" experience:

"I was born in Amherst County in 1927. At that time, there was no high school in my area. We had one room schools. I went to Cedar Knob from one to seventh grade. We had to walk from my father's farm to where the school was. We walked two-and a-half to three miles, one way. I was six years old. You can imagine a six-year-old girl walking through the snow sometimes almost up to her waist! My older half-brothers used to pick me up and take me to school.

"The sad thing about that was, we had buses that were coming up the same road that I had to walk, picking up all the White kids and taking them to a White school which was called Pleasant View. And I never, never understood how in the world they could pass us, splashing mud and snow. The bus was empty when it was going up the road. They passed my brothers and myself, just walking. I just wonder why we couldn't have ridden that bus."

Ed told a story of a friend, an older woman, a member of his church, who had known him and his family for years.

"We were coming out of church one Sunday morning, and [this friend] said, 'I want to speak to you.'

"And I said, 'Well, certainly. What's up?'

"And she said, 'Why in hell are you sending your daughter to E. C. Glass? I just wonder what you all could be thinking about! You know it's wrong to send her.'

"And this was a Black lady! And that lady has gone to her grave; she's probably looking down at me telling that story now. But she knows I am telling the truth! She stopped speaking to me! She never had any more time for me and she had always talked to me. She stopped speaking to me and had no use for me after that.

"Now that's my own kind. So what can I expect from my White brothers?"

What did *I* expect from my White brothers and sisters? As this leading unfolded, and I continued to read and to learn about the civil rights movement, racism, and White privilege, I cringed at what was so often wreaked upon the world by White people: in our name.

Dimly I understood that much of my cringing was about what *I* had perpetuated. Because of my blindness to my own stuff, for example, my first draft had proved so painful for Lynda and Owen. Dimly I understood that before I could truly be open to whatever it was Spirit wanted me to do, I had to forgive myself. Dimly I understood that those ugly qualities listed on the "White Supremacy Culture" handout *were* me, no matter how hard I tried to convince myself and everyone else—you, for example—that I was an enlightened anti-racist. But how to get past my shame, my anger? How easily I could imagine myself on that White bus, blithely riding past Georgia and her brothers!

At another time in my life, when my own stuff, some of it acquired during my adolescent years in Lynchburg, was blocking my spiritual path, an experience at Boston's Isabella Stewart Gardner Museum helped to open the way. Although I had been a member of Cambridge Meeting for many years, there were elements of my faith which still remained confusing. What was my relationship with Jesus *Christ*, for example? Because of my Unitarian-Universalist background, what I'd absorbed from my parents and from Sunday schools in the North and in Lynchburg, the word "Christ" stuck in my throat.

Yet I knew that good people, people of faith, righteous people, people who both talked the talk *and* walked the walk loved this Jesus Christ, this holy man from Nazareth, this "Jesus, the carpenter's son." One of my own students from Cambridge Meeting's high school class had stood up in the balcony one Sunday morning and talked about reading the New Testament. "I love that Jesus," she exclaimed. How could I connect with that love, so powerful, so transformational in her life and in the lives of millions of people? How could I get past my own stuckness around the word "Christ?"

A small and exquisite painting at the Gardner Museum pointed the way. Not a Biblical scholar, I could not identify most of the women in the painting, shown at the foot of the cross, cradling Jesus's body just after the crucifixion. But having just read a fascinating book about Mary Magdalene and how her "story" has changed over time as Western culture's view of women changes, I happened to know that, often, Mary Magdalene has been depicted as a redhead. And, yes, there she was, Mary Magdalene, her flame-colored tresses flowing over her robe, tenderly holding Jesus.

Mary Magdalene, whom Jesus first entrusted with the news of his resurrection, loved him, I thought. And so does my First Day School student. And so do so many people I admire. I can reach Jesus *Christ* through the love of others. That's my way in.

On that Hurricane Jeanne trip, it was three extraordinary White women, none of them redheads, all three of them born and raised in the South, who showed me the way through my own stuff, my own imperfections, my own racism, my own propensity to judge, my own fears, towards reconciliation with my own kind. Thus, I discovered what John Woolman discovered while following *his* leadings: that seemingly random encounters with people along the way are very much a part of any spiritual journey.

One of the many lessons this leading has taught me is that most people do not share my Spirit-led zeal. Family, friends, members of my faith community, while supportive and willing to listen as I regale them—at some length—about the most recent stop along this spiritual journey, have generally not been the key people who might help to move this process along. Like Blanche DuBois, I have had to rely on the kindness of strangers, strangers busy with the concerns of their own lives and who, therefore, do not feel a need to reply to my letters, phone calls, or e-mails. So when Joyce Maddox, the office manager for Lynchburg's Warwick House Publishing, called to say she might be able to help locate Owen's father's manuscript, I was astonished that she had even returned my phone call.

Because O. C. Cardwell's manuscript promised to illuminate much about Lynchburg's civil rights movement, locating "No Matter How Long" had assumed enormous significance, a quest to find The Holy Grail. Owen, who had no clear idea where his father's work might be, had offered a few possibilities. Most of them proved dead ends. Way opened with one suggestion, however: Remembering that his father had hoped to get his manuscript published, Owen suggested I try Warwick House, Lynchburg's self-publishing firm. After she had called to say she might be able to help, Warwick House's Joyce Maddox called Owen to verify who I was. She then called me again, this time to report that "No Matter How Long" languished on a Warwick House shelf and in short order arranged for me to receive a disk of this precious manuscript.

Enormously grateful for her help, my gratitude grew as Joyce and I continued to talk on the phone. Born and raised in the South, witness to the civil rights movement, steeped in Lynchburg history, Joyce candidly shared her own experiences of Lynchburg during the fifties, sixties, and seventies. *Her* conversations with Leighton Dodd, former mayor of Lynchburg, with whom she had worked before coming to Warwick House, had opened her eyes to systemic racism, she told me. On her own, Joyce mailed back issues of *Lynch's Ferry*, a journal of Lynchburg history also published by Warwick Press, which she thought might be helpful to my work.

It was during a brief visit with the attractive, trim Joyce that I learned how she extended her kindness and going-that-extra-mile to others besides myself. Heavy rains from Hurricane Jeanne pounding outside, Joyce and I met for the first time face-to-face in her high-ceilinged, busy office in the John Marshall Warwick House. Once an elegant private home, built in 1826, Warwick House is one of a row of hand-some, two-story, brick, antebellum homes located on Court Street, just a few blocks from Court Street Baptist Church.

After an older man came by to drop off a manuscript for her to proofread, she explained that on any given day, many downtown residents, some of them homeless or living in near-by rooming houses, dropped by the office to tell their stories. "You would not believe what I have heard," she exclaimed in her lilting voice. From Warwick House patrons, who could afford to pay to have their memoirs and family histories pub-lished, Joyce had learned the power of the personal narrative. So even though it often meant that she took her work home to complete, Joyce willingly listened to some of Lynchburg's most indigent residents relate their life stories.

"We can do no great things," Mother Teresa once said, "only small things with great love." Joyce Maddox's patient, compassionate listening and her willingness to examine her "white southern tribal values" have illuminated, for me, just what Mother Teresa meant.

✦

"Are you a scholar?" Carolyn Bell quizzed me during our first phone conversation. How should I respond? If defined as someone eagerly and doggedly seeking knowledge, then, yes, I was a scholar. Surely the hours I spent at Harvard's Widener Library, for example, surrounded by bona fide scholars, por-ing over old issues of the South's most influential African

American newspaper, *The Norfolk Journal and Guide,* qualified me as a scholar?

But then again, surely a true scholar knew how to keep track of information better than I. She would have understood how important it was to get her hands on Lynchburg's desegregation-case court documents and how to find those documents. She wouldn't lose notes or, as happened during the most recent interview with Owen and Lynda, would make *absolutely sure* the tape recorder was working properly. Would a true scholar indulge in time-consuming detours to read more on topics she simply found fascinating? And wouldn't a *real* scholar disdain books altogether and seek primary sources?

"No," I answered truthfully. "I'm not a scholar." Why is this woman, a complete stranger, asking me this? I then wondered huffily. What a rude question!

"If you were a scholar," Carolyn Bell explained, "you would be eligible to apply for a Virginia Foundation for the Humanities grant."

Oh, I suddenly realized, she's trying to help me!

Randolph-Macon professor and member of the Legacy Museum's board, Carolyn Bell proved enormously helpful to my leading. As she and I became better acquainted, I learned that she was writing a history of Randolph-Macon Woman's College. "I just knew one chapter had to be about race," the Louisiana native explained. Her interest in this weighty subject led her to the Legacy Museum of African American History where she quickly became a sort of volunteer administrator. It was in this capacity that she had first called in response to a letter I had sent the museum.

Although by the time Carolyn Bell and I first spoke, intimations of where this leading might be actually leading seemed slightly more clear—*something* about young people, *something* other than a book, perhaps *something* about prison ministry?—I still flailed about. While expectantly waiting and urged to do so by Owen, I began looking into grants to cover travel expenses for the three of us. In pursuit of a possible grant from the Virginia Foundation for the Humanities (VFH), I had contacted the Legacy Museum; Carolyn Bell responded to my query. By the end of the Randolph-Macon professor's and my initial conversation, it was clear that not only was I *not* a scholar but that the VFH, which only awarded grants to scholars, already gave substantial grants to the Legacy Museum itself. So even if we could somehow get around the scholar requirement—after all, Lynda was a Ph.D.—a grant application from Owen, Lynda, and me would be in competition with an established and exemplary Lynchburg organization. Our success seemed unlikely.

Equally unlikely, given her considerable teaching and Legacy Museum responsibilities, was that Carolyn Bell would find the time to meet me early one morning at the Legacy Museum, on a day when the museum was closed to the public, show me a wealth of materials, and then, in the midst of countless other demands—including Parents Weekend—return a few days later to see how I was doing and to answer my questions. But she did.

That same day Carolyn had come to check up on me, the college professor had attended a lecture on Sally Hemmings at Thomas Jefferson's Monticello in Charlottesville, Virginia, and had been the only White person in attendance. When the lecturer had asked the group which branch of Sally Hemmings's descendants, the ones who for generations had been passing for White or the ones who identified themselves as African American, had requested to be buried at Monticello, Carolyn Bell had been the only person in the room who had not known the answer. The White branch, families accustomed to getting what they wanted, had insisted on the Monticello burial, she explained to me.

Of course I hadn't known the answer, either.

"There's that privilege again," I noted. Carolyn Bell agreed.

✦

One of the many Legacy Museum treasures Carolyn Bell shared with me was a cardboard box full of tapes she'd recorded when working on the race chapter for her book. The box included her interviews with Lynchburg civil rights leaders, Virgil Wood and Olivet Thaxton, and several tapes of a lengthy interview with Rebecca Owen.

In December of 1960, six college students, White and Black, conducted Lynchburg's first sit-in. Students from Randolph-Macon Woman's College, Lynchburg College, and Virginia Seminary and College sat together at Patterson's Drug Store lunch counter for which the sit-inners were arrested, tried, and sentenced to thirty days in jail. One of the six had been Rebecca Owen, a senior at the all-White Randolph-Macon. [Lynchburg College was also all-White at that time; Virginia Seminary and College students were African American.] Listening to the Rebecca Owen interview, I quickly realized that her story had little to do with my research. Yet I ignored the pile of much more relevant materials on a Legacy Museum table to listen to Rebecca Owen's tired, sad voice for hours, only taking a ten-minute break to enjoy a brief, carefree ride on the Old City Cemetery's pecan-tree swing.

What did I hear that was so compelling? Here was a young woman, born and raised in a small coastal Virginia town, a member of a Virginian family and a member of an established, socially-acceptable religious denomination, who found Randolph-Macon's "plantation" culture confusing and alien and its emphasis on ladylike behavior equally baffling. "If *she* was confused," I wrote in my journal, "this brilliant, southern, exposed-to-the-progressive-ideas-floating-around-at-that-time, spiritual person, what hope did I have? Her activism, spiritually based, was not supported [neither by Randolph-Macon nor her Methodist church]. So much pain. Knowing that she died of cancer a year and a half ago makes her voice more sorrowful, more reflective, than it already was."

Until listening to Rebecca Owen, one of the stories I had always told myself was that if I had been born into an established Virginian family, had attended the same church many of my E. C. Glass classmates attended, had done better in school—in other words, had been more like Rebecca Owen—I would have known how to be "a white child-woman" in Lynchburg, Virginia, in the late fifties, early sixties. But Rebecca Owen had been just as baffled and confused by the expected "ladylike" role as I.

After I became a Quaker and began to understand how my spiritual life underpinned my political activism, I decided that had my Lynchburg U-U church been more politically active, I would have confidently walked over to that high school cafeteria table where Owen sat on January 29, 1962, and struck up a conversation with him. For this daring action, I told myself, I would have found inspiration and support from my faith community.

"Daddy blamed the Methodist Church when I, a white child-woman, age twenty, was arrested in Lynchburg, Virginia," the sit-inner noted. It was not Rebecca's church in Saluda her father blamed—"At Christmas communion service [shortly after the sit-in] at my home church, almost no one spoke to me,"—nor the Methodist-affiliated Randolph-Macon Woman's College that Mr. Owen decried. (Clearly still bitter, Rebecca Owen spoke at great length about her alma mater's lack of support.) Rebecca Owen's active participation in the civil rights movement had been inspired by a Methodist youth forum on civil rights she attended the summer of 1960. Like Rosa Parks, whose Highlander Folk School experience at a race relations workshop paved the way for her historic action on a Montgomery bus, Rebecca Owen's decision to join a drug store sit-in had been nurtured and encouraged by her attendance at that Methodist youth forum. It wasn't my Lynchburg U-U church's failure to be more politically active that kept me from walking over to Owen that day, I realized. Because I had never attended any U-U-sponsored race rela-tions workshops or civil rights forums, I was unprepared, untrained, unconnected.

Because she was still working on her own book, Carolyn Bell asked that I not quote from her taped material. But an entire chapter in *Journeys That Opened Up the World: Women, Student Christian Movements, and Social Justice, 1955-1975* was devoted to Rebecca Owen. Here are Rebecca Owen's words from another source:

When she was twelve years old and living with her family in Saluda, Virginia, Rebecca Owen had her "first inkling that the gospel was revolutionary." After meeting Methodist Youth Fellowship leaders and outspoken missionaries and anti-poverty workers at Methodist-sponsored conferences, the Randolph-Macon scholarship student became convinced that "the mores of my well-bred southern white tribe seemed not only unjust but archaic and absurd."

While in a Lynchburg jail, Rebecca wrote to her family:

Reading nothing but the Bible and Bonhoeffer [a German theologian hanged for his attempt to assassinate Hitler], I'm getting pretty steeped in [Christian] thought. I'll have to be careful to do nothing radical when I get out. I think the Bible is probably the most revolutionary book I've read...One thing that has struck me is what a privileged person I am from the fact of my birth and environment. This position is something we cannot escape and perhaps it is the greatest stumbling-block in our way to understanding Christianity. Jesus certainly did not come to the privileged of his day primarily, and those of position were least able to hear him. This is a burden we must bear and it is amazing to me that I had been so oblivious to it before.

Rebecca Owen, an extraordinary woman whose courage, brilliance, and religious faith were undeniable, provided the larger, historical context for my Cold War, Jim Crow, pre-woman's movement-era adolescence. For which I am most grateful.

NOTES: In Our Name

p. 151. Mary Magdalene
Imagine my astonishment when I realized that *Swimming In It* was simply another installment of the Mary Magdalene tale! Red-

headed Jewell, a one-time prostitute, homeless, ill, and desperate, arrives at a homeless shelter run by Quakers. *Swimming In It* traces Jewell's first, tentative steps toward self-reliance and her spiritual awakening.

p. 152. Leighton Dodd

On March 9, 1971, city councilman and prominent 03-er, Leighton Dodd made a pivotal speech: "Although everyone is talking about the schools, I can't help but feel that they are not the real problem but are just a symptom of a much larger problem—that being the lack of understanding and trust between both blacks and whites…What I am saying in a very personal way is that I have assumed that progress between blacks and whites was someone else's problem…Only by being totally honest with each other can we create mutual trust."

For this speech, Leighton Dodd and his family suffered a cross to be burned on their lawn.

pp. 153, 154. *The Norfolk Journal and Guide*

As bona fide scholar Henry Lewis Suggs discovered, the history of Black-owned newspapers in the South is rich material and their contents fascinating to read. As noted before, the present-day editor of *The Norfolk Journal and Guide* is Brenda Hughes Andrews (who once ate a piece of watermelon off a White demonstrator's plate at the S&W Cafeteria.)

Henry Lewis Suggs, editor, *The Black Press in the South, 1865-1979*. Suggs also wrote a book about *The Norfolk Journal and Guide's* former editor: *P. B. Young, Newspaperman: Race, Politics, and Journalism in the New South, 1910 –1962*.

p. 154. Randolph-Macon Woman's College:

In September of 2006, the trustees of Randolph-Macon announced that the prestigious woman's college is slated to become co-ed in 2007 and renamed Randolph College.

p. 154. Dr. Bell has subsequently retired.

p. 157. The Highlander Folk School:

Rosa Parks attended this school, located in Monteagle, Tennessee, where she learned about the non-violent movement in the summer of 1955.

✦

Jackson, MS, 1966
by Howard Levy

When she suddenly said "jump," holding on
to the old woman's hand, not letting go at all
though the old woman was anxious to get away
from us, the trouble we brought, the mixing up
of settled things, the warm February air
of Mississippi seemed to me to collaborate,
to sustain our white college boy
arms and heads higher and longer than possible.

Mrs. Carolyn Williams, two hundred pounds if a one,
just back to her native Jackson
after the poison of Chicago, grown huge
with her appetite for change, knew
this one would never register to vote,
70, a retarded daughter in tow, scared
even by a knock at her door,
one Negro woman, two white men,
since white folks on her dirt street only meant pain,
or viciousness, the bill collectors or the police,
but still deserved a treat, a gift of a moment in the future
and a joke on the rotted past.

And so when the old woman asked which of the two white men
was in charge, Mrs. Williams just turned to us
and ordered "Jump" and we jumped:
the Red Sea didn't part, the Confederate
flag didn't come down from the gold-domed Capitol
and what changed was just enough in the woman's eyes
and Mrs. Williams released her.

✦

Reprinted by permission.

CHAPTER 11
Just Enough

Again, but this time for the last time, way opened because of a grant application. In December of 2004, I won an Arts Lottery grant from the Somerville Arts Council which required grant recipients to share our work with Somerville residents. Although I'm usually organized when it comes to deadlines and due dates, for some reason, the time for me to submit my community-benefit proposal, in which I was to explain to the Arts Council how I planned to share my work with Somerville residents, came and went. A firm but polite e-mail from the Arts Council forced me to quickly come up with an idea.

Something about young people: Since this leading seemed, in part, about "the passing on of what I know, what I've experienced to my sphere of influence" to youth, as Owen had said, I decided my community-benefit audience should be Somerville High School students. Thus I made an appointment to speak with Joseph Burke, the head of the History Department for the Somerville Public Schools. Delicious smells wafting from Somerville High School's cafeteria, the memory of another high school and another cafeteria foremost in my mind, I sat with Mr. Burke in the teachers' dining room and as efficiently as I could, explained why I was there.

Knowing how harried school administrators are and knowing that he and I both understood that the only reason I had asked to meet with him was so I could collect my grant money, I had expected Mr. Burke to distractedly—perhaps rudely—listen and then, if I were lucky, find a way to accommodate my need. To my surprise, however, the first thing the indeed busy Mr. Burke did was to ask me to tell him more! GE transferring six-hundred families from upstate NY to sleepy Lynchburg. How the city got its name. Virginia's massive resistance. Lynda and Owen's story.

"Your work fits nicely with our 'Facing History and Ourselves' classes," Mr. Burke told me. "Would you be willing to speak to them?" Instantly I agreed. Had I known this meant I was to speak to five classes and that Somerville High School classes are sixty-six minutes long, I might have reconsidered.

◆

Scenarios: What would you do?

Questions to consider:
- *Do we have enough information?*
- *What's the historical context? (pretty much the same question as #1!)*
- *Did everyone in the group have an opportunity to share his/her opinion?*

Scene One:
You're seventeen. You're White. You grew up in the North but now you're a senior in an all-White public high school in a segregated southern city; you've been attending this high school since tenth grade. Today is January 29, 1962, the first day that two African American students, a boy and a girl, have begun classes at your school. Because they are freshmen and you are a senior, you haven't seen these new students all morning, but now it's lunch time and your friends have told you that the African American boy just got into the cafeteria line. You spot him approaching a table where four or five White boys sit; the table is near where you are standing. The seated boys jump up; the African American student sits down by himself.
What do you do?

Scene Two:
You're fifteen. You're the only African American male in a Virginian high school with over two-thousand White students. Today is November 22, 1963; John F. Kennedy, the president of the United States, has just been assassinated. You're walking down the

hallway between classes and a young man behind you yells, "They killed your hero, didn't they?" You spin around and hit the guy.

What do you do now?

[from the booklet I prepared for Somerville High School students]

"Facing History and Ourselves" asks students to grapple with moral and ethical questions: What would you do if the Nazis came to your German village and began rounding up all the Jews? By day two of my presentations at Somerville High School, it dawned on me that I, too, was facing history and myself. Here I am, I realized, old enough to be a grandmother and I'm discussing real-life scenarios with students the same age Owen and I had been when these incidents actually occurred.

Demographically, the 115 students I faced represented a far different population than the 1962 E. C. Glass High School's solidly middle-class, 99.9 percent White make-up. Although in recent years more affluent people have bought homes and condominiums in Somerville, most of these more wealthy newcomers either do not have children or choose to send their children to private school. Thus, to a significant degree, Somerville's public high school reflects the city's former history when only poor Whites, the working-class, and recent immigrants lived in the city.

For two days SHS American History classes, their racial mix mirroring Somerville's diversity, chewed over the two scenarios I had prepared for them. With candor and passion when discussing the first incident, they talked about what it means to be different, about "doing the right thing," about peer pressure and the fears of being an outcast, about the possible danger involved if a White girl sat down beside an African American boy in 1962 in a city named *Lynch*burg, Virginia. "Of course I'd go sit with that guy," some students said confidently. Others challenged that statement.

Reaction to the second scenario revealed that at least at Somerville High School, and at least among some of the young male students willing to voice their opinion, there has been a dramatic shift in high school culture: "Once you start

163

something," these young men explained to me patiently, "you have to finish it." In other words, you cannot just "hit the guy" and walk away. (There were many students, male and female, it should be noted, who simply answered, "Run!") When told that Owen's guidance counselor had made the incident "go away," students, regardless of gender, were incredulous. "That guidance counselor must have had a lot of power," an Hispanic young man opined.

That not one Somerville High student thought to ask for help from faculty—or any other adult—begged me to look at the original scenario with a fresh eye. I realized that Owen, accustomed to the tightly knit, supportive Dunbar High, had, by immediately seeking out GC's help, replicated a pattern he had known and cherished and benefited from at his former, all-Black school. How fortunate that the White adult Owen went to that day, the day President Kennedy had been assassinated, had been able to put aside whatever feelings that tragedy stirred up, and to so effectively respond to Owen's need. How fortunate that GC had been worthy of that young man's trust!

By day two at Somerville High, deeply moved, this "guilty White woman" was thanking those students for this incredible opportunity to face a pivotal experience in my own life. Unfailingly polite, the students received my thanks with grace and good humor.

✦

Although deeply moved by those students' grace and good humor, I was chagrined to realize how badly I'd planned my presentation. Looking into the faces of those Haitian, Brazilian, El Salvadoran, and White students, what I should have anticipated beforehand became clear: race was a charged topic for those young people. Yet I had allotted so little time for any such discussion. Before my presentation, the school's sixty-six minute classes had seemed alarmingly ample. But, I quickly saw, when it comes to the subject of race, there's never enough time.

My observations at Somerville High School left me with a question: What did Lynda and Owen's story mean to *Lynchburg's* current students? While I had observed a racially-mixed E. C. Glass High School when Lynda, Owen, and I had last visited our alma mater, I knew nothing of those students' day-to-day experience of race. And, remembering the stories told at Cambridge Rindge and Latin's race forum, I knew that even in the most seemingly enlightened public high school in one of the most seemingly enlightened communities in this country, much was hidden, much was left unsaid.

I remembered, too, my asinine question during that race forum to that young man in the Malcolm X tee shirt. As awkward as that moment was, hadn't I been fuzzily intuiting how little I knew of today's students' knowledge of the civil rights movement? By asking that stunningly stupid question, hadn't I been asking him to tell me what he knew? What did today's E. C. Glass students know of Lynda and Owen's historical context?

After a period of discernment, I decided to contact the city's newly appointed superintendent of schools, Dr. Paul McKendrick. In my letter I sought permission—incredibly naively, I now realize—to interview Lynchburg high school students. Dr. McKendrick, the city's first African American superintendent of schools, did not reply to my letter nor to subsequent phone calls, however.

Discouraged, I nevertheless continued to pray over this. There's something here, my Inner Voice whispered. So I gave over my own willing, gave over my own running, gave over my own desiring to know or be anything and sank down to that seed which God sowed in my heart.

Of course Dr. McKendrick wouldn't respond; it finally came to me. To him, I was a stranger and a Yankee, a complete unknown who, out of the blue proposed to talk about the charged subject of race with Lynchburg high school students. In the superintendent's eyes, I was perhaps no different, in some ways, from those "outside agitators" of the civil rights movement!

The semi-ironic words of a former boss, when she hired me to teach adult learners, came to me: "What you should be doing," Susan Lane Riley explained, "is asking 'How best may I serve?' " I should be *asking* Lynchburg school officials—administrators in charge of curriculum, perhaps?—how best may I serve? I should ask how my homework for this leading might prove helpful.

And way opened:

"I can tell you that your work does dovetail nicely with the Standards of Learning for high school Virginia and United States History," Susan White, supervisor for instruction for the Lynchburg City Schools wrote in May of 2005. "...Our teachers are always looking for resources to make history come alive for their students, and it seems to me from your time line [I'd mailed a copy of my Somerville High School booklet to the director of curriculum] that your project may do just that. So I look forward to hearing from you and beginning our conversation."

What is this Standards of Learning, better known as SOLs? SOLs is a statewide, "high-stakes," standardized, multiple-choice test, much like Massachusetts' MCAS. Beginning in 2004, Virginia's public school students must pass at least six of the eleven SOL tests in order to graduate. Some critics of this test—and there are many—claim that SOLs had been created by former Virginia Governor George Allen and other like-minded politicians to undermine public education and to create support for charter schools and vouchers. As happens in Massachusetts, students in poor school districts—like Somerville, Massachusetts, or Virginia's Prince Edward County—score less well on these state-mandated standardized tests than in more affluent communities. Fundamental questions concerning *who* decides what body of information is to be learned for these tests have been raised. Are the contributions of women and people of color included in the World and U.S. History tests, for example? And, as also happens in

Massachusetts, many Virginia teachers and administrators feel they spend too much time "teaching to the test" and not enough time on, say, critical thinking skills or enrichment.

Or that all-important subject of race in the classroom. Ann Marie Smith, an adjunct professor at the University of Maryland, interviewed five history teachers at an unnamed Virginia high school to ascertain how SOLs impacted their teaching methods. One, "Mrs. Hanson," taught a senior-level elective called "Minority Cultures." "Every year I have to fight to keep this class," stated Mrs. Hanson. "The administrators don't see this as an important class, but these students work well together in here—they make a lot of friends in this class that they normally wouldn't." The history teacher went on to say:

> Well, I have very little in the way of respect for the SOLs, to tell you the truth. I feel that the SOLs were developed and provided by a bunch of people who are white, middle-class—and came out of the school of the fifties. And I think they purposely tried to bring all of that time period back because it enhances one group's power, I suppose.

The impact of these tests cannot be overstated. During our first telephone conversation to discuss how best I might serve, Susan White used the words *Civil War*. Now, I knew many things had changed in the South since my very first day at E. C. Glass when, after saying "Civil War," a Yankee-hating classmate had snapped, "There wasn't anything civil about it!" Nevertheless, Ms. White's usage seemed so remarkable that I interrupted her to comment on her word choice.

"My husband still says 'The War of Northern Aggression.'" she sighed. "But SOLs says Civil War. So that's what I say."

◆

"You want me to do *what*?" others have asked incredulously when faced with what seemed impossible or out-of-left field promptings from Spirit. So when this leading seemed to be taking a sharp, unexpected turn towards *curriculum development* in relation to a high performance test, I was both incredulous and leery: "You want me to do *what?* I don't even know what 'scope and sequence' mean!"

But then I would think about what "Mrs. Hanson" had said about the SOLs.

> Well, I have very little in the way of respect for the SOLs to tell you the truth. I feel that the SOLs were developed and provided by a bunch of people who are white, middle-class—and came out of the school of the fifties....

You want me to do *what*? What was I getting myself into?

But then I'd think about Owen's comment: "I don't want our picture to be just another picture hanging. The kids who were in those two sessions [when he and Lynda spoke at E. C. Glass] got something. What about the rest of the school?"

Or Lynda's response when asked: "Did you ever feel that your presence in E. C. Glass meant that people were actually talking and learning from one another?"

"No way did that happen!" Lynda had responded heatedly. "*We* learned. I think they actively tried not to."

We learned, Lynda Woodruff had said. Because, praise Spirit, Lynda and Owen were willing to trust me, I have begun to learn.

Was I being nudged to share what I am learning with Lynchburg Public School students? Perhaps. But, I'd think, looking at all the books on Lynchburg history sitting on my shelf: How?

NOTES: Just Enough

p. 167. Standards of Learning Tests:

Much of the information on SOLs comes from a 2003 paper by Ann Marie Smith: "Negotiating Control and Protecting the Private: History Teachers and the Virginia Standards of Learning."

✦

You must be the change you wish to see in the world.
—*Mahatma Gandhi*

✦

CHAPTER 12
Changes

In 1983, about a year after I joined Friends Meeting at Cambridge, I took a break from my parenting responsibilities for four daughters—a teenager, a two-year-old, and newborn twins—to spend a delightful afternoon with my then-husband's friend, the animator Lisa Crafts. Lisa and her partner and fellow animator Ken Brown lived in a funky, spacious, art-filled apartment on Inman Street in Cambridge. This early spring day outing had been initiated by my husband, who was out of work at the time. "I'll watch the kids," he offered. "You need to be with another woman artist for a while." For he had noticed that I became less frantic, less snappish, less anxious, less *crazed* when I found brief, sporadic moments in which to write during that challenging period.

Lisa fed me, I remember, something delicious, something artfully arranged. (Within weeks of Ken and Lisa's subsequent move to the Tribeca section of Manhattan, *The New Yorker* raved about one of Lisa's food presentations in its "Talk of the Town" section.) She showed me drawings from the animated film she was currently working on. We discussed the film's story line, her upcoming projects.

"Don't you think it's strange that we have separate, different words for art and sex and love and life?" she asked me, her lovely face lit with passion.

I had no idea what she meant.

Twenty-one years later, I understand. My four daughters successfully launched, in a loving, supportive relationship, my financial situation stable, so many precious things in my life seem inexorably entwined, seamless: my writing, my spiritual practice, yoga, my marriage, the books I take out from the library, the monthly meetings with Susan Lloyd and Wendy, long meditative walks.

But was I "walking the walk?" How did spending hours writing in the comfort of my home, or attending a yoga class, or reading another insightful book on racism square with the quote from Micah taped on my computer: "The Lord God has told us what is right and what he demands: See that justice be done, let mercy be your first concern, and humbly obey your God."

During my early morning yoga class, for example, in a second-story studio right in my own neighborhood, as morning-rush-hour traffic on Somerville Avenue streamed by, I'd sometimes hear an 87 bus stop below the studio's front windows. Waiting for that bus in rain, sleet, and snow were my neighbors, I knew, many of them from El Salvador, Haiti, recent arrivals from Brazil, on their way to low-paying, dead-end jobs, perhaps the first of several jobs they would trudge to that day. Although I understand that caring for my aging body is essential, still, there have been times when I would emerge from the yoga studio, flush with some personal breakthrough I had achieved that morning to see those waiting bus travelers and wonder: Does my ability to do an assisted backbend further the causes of justice and mercy?

A small act: About two years ago, I "came out" as a Quaker in my every-other-weekly column for *The Somerville Journal* in the belief that voices from the Religious Left should be heard in the current, ongoing public discourse in this country. This Quaker self-identification seemed a small gesture, however, an insignificant drop in the "ocean of darkness," and, like writing a check for the American Friends Service Committee or Amnesty International, performed without personal risk. For surely "walking the walk" asks for a kind of spiritual backbend. Surely justice can be done and mercy be our first concern when we, with Divine Assistance, face something hard, perform something challenging, move towards a perhaps frightening "growing edge," as Cambridge Meeting's resident Friend, Tom Ash, has often said.

An ugly incident and its aftermath in Somerville produced such a heart-racing moment for me. I relate this story not to put myself forward as a superior White woman but to illustrate a moment when my writing life, my spiritual practice, my leading, and the Micah 6:8 enjoinder entwined:

A few years ago, for many reasons, a terrifying gang known as MS-13 established itself in Somerville (population 77,000). Born out of the violence and chaos of the El Salvadoran civil war and its Death Squads, via the mean streets of Los Angeles, in recent years MS-13 has become a powerful, much-feared, coast-to-coast gang. Although the gang's arrival in East Somerville, where the majority of Somerville's El Salvadoran residents live, had certainly come to the notice of that area's residents, the rest of the city was unaware of MS-13's existence, let alone its presence in our hometown. But when a reputed MS-13 gang member allegedly raped a young, disabled girl in an East Somerville park, everyone in Somerville, especially young women, took notice.

Somerville politicians, in response to understandable and vociferous public outrage, began to craft an "Anti-Gang Ordinance" which, they claimed, the Somerville Police Department had begged for in order to counter MS-13. This proposed ordinance would allow the police to arrest gang members—or, at least, young men the police believed to be gang members—who loitered in public places. The ordinance was quickly labeled "racial-profiling" by the city's El Salvadoran leaders.

When a public hearing on this proposed ordinance was announced, I knew the "public" who would show up at City Hall—members of the city's El Salvadoran community and one or two progressive, ACLU-member lawyers. In a moment of clarity, however, the word "witness" came to me. Sometimes, it is "just enough" to simply show up, I realized. So I did.

At the hearing, several Somerville aldermen, members of the Public Safety Committee—one of whom was a woman, none of whom were El Salvadoran—sat around a large table in the aldermen's meeting room; seated with these aldermen was Somerville's burly chief of police.

The group surrounding the aldermen's table was composed, indeed, of El Salvadoran citizens and a couple of activist lawyers. In addition, the group included someone I had *not* predicted but, given her proclivities, probably should have; let's call her Mrs. Lowell. An older White woman who spoke with a deep, gravelly, slightly accented voice and who, it is rumored, was related by marriage to one of Massachusetts' most prominent families, Mrs. Lowell, always in a hat and suit, patrolled City Hall by day and night. Often mistaken for an elected official because of her formal attire and her liberal use of the aldermanic copy machine, Mrs. Lowell was an expected but not always welcomed attendee at City Hall gatherings.

As I found a chair against the wall, that "White Supremacy Culture" handout came to mind. If I am to properly function as a White witness, I thought, then I should, indeed, embrace the tenets of my culture. So this Worshipper of The Written Word pulled out a notebook and pen from my bag and began taking careful notes. Thus, as the meeting progressed, I noticed when the chief of police contradicted himself. Asked about a key piece of this proposed ordinance, the chief had responded to the same question in two completely opposite ways.

After the aldermen—and woman—had politely listened to the police chief and asked questions, members of the public were given an opportunity to speak. Several of us indicated we had something to say; Tom Taylor, the alderman from Ward 3 and someone I know slightly, established the order: "…and then Mrs. Lowell, and then you, Patricia."

Predictably, the El Salvadoran residents and the lawyers, while condemning the violence perpetuated by MS-13, voiced their grave concern that the proposed ordinance was both racist and unconstitutional. Unpredictably, however, when it was Mrs. Lowell's turn to speak, she spewed forth an anti-immigrant invective, nastily castigating anyone who spoke Spanish.

Primed for a Gotcha! moment with the police chief about his contradictory statements, when it was my turn, I didn't know what to say for a few seconds. But Mrs. Lowell's comments had been so outrageous, I knew such nastiness had to be immediately repudiated. Indeed, as another White woman, although my racing heart told me how uncomfortable, how anxious this repudiation made me, it was my responsibility to do so. I prayed for the right words:

"I do not share the previous speaker's views," I said firmly. "In fact, I find them deeply troubling."

✦

August 2005, at the Kentucky State Fair:

It's a steamy morning in Louisville so the four of us—my husband, his daughter, Jess, her boyfriend, Eric, and I—immediately head for the air-conditioned farming exhibitions. Too late for the rooster-crowing preliminaries, we file up and down rows of caged poultry, inspect the rabbits, then move on. We chat with beekeepers and buy honey and aromatic beeswax candles. Peering over a tall, white-painted fence, we watch skittish Holsteins, their udders seemingly about to burst as they, commandeered by their husky owners, slowly and reluctantly circle a sawdusty ring. Why one sheaf of tobacco or ear of corn is better than its peers is not immediately apparent and our ignorance humbles us. After studying the accompanying explanation to the prize-winning bale of hay, however (figures which explain how well the sweet-smelling hay will feed livestock), we understand why that particular bale deserved its shiny blue ribbon.

An exhibit sponsored by the Kentucky Farm Bureau catches our eye; horrified, the four of us move closer. Looming above us is an actual tractor cradled by a large steel device which, clicking and whirring, tilts the entire tractor to its side every few seconds, then rights the farm vehicle again. What captures our attention to this dangers-of-tractor-rollovers display is neither the shiny red tractor nor the clicking, whirring machine but the human-sized dummy seated in the tractor seat, its bobbling head knocked against the tilting machine's steel side again and again and again. The dummy is Black.

I look around me; the crowd around us is overwhelmingly White. Images from the Without Sanctuary exhibit leap to mind: Photographs of crowds of leering, jovial Whites in the foreground while behind them a lifeless Black figure dangles from a tall tree. My stomach churning, I turn to my step-daughter: "I'm going to say something."

Jess looks at me with concern. "All right," the Earlham College graduate says hesitantly.

Briskly I walk over to a table placed to the side of the tractor display where sit three young White Farm Bureau employees, two women and a man, in identical polo shirts. "Good morning," the young man drawls, giving me a prize-winning smile. "Nice day, innit."

Not a stranger to Southern-conversation opening remarks, nevertheless I plunge immediately into what I have to say: "I'm from Boston," I blurt out, "and I—"

The young man interrupts: "'Scuse me; Boston, *Massachusetts*? Because we have a Boston here, you know."

Somehow I know I should pay close attention to that proud "we" but recklessly continue. "Yes. Boston, Mass.," I crisply respond. "I'm looking at these exhibits and seeing what Kentucky is saying about itself. And I have to tell you: the fact that your display's dummy is African American I find deeply offensive."

"But it's not," one woman argues.

Her instant, earnest response seems, at first, defensive but then, suddenly, a faint inner-warning sounds: Perhaps you're being too quick to judge, it whispers.

Whether trained to placate people like me or just naturally charming, the young man assures me that I am not the first person at the fair to bring this to the Farm Bureau's attention. "We have another dummy on order," he says. Soothed by this, I thank the trio for their attention and rejoin our little group.

But something nags at me. "Can I process that conversation with you?" I ask my stepdaughter as we admire rows of colorful, handcrafted quilts. "There's something about it that just sits wrong."

"Sure," she says gently. All it takes is one, deep look into her wise-beyond-her-years brown eyes, and I immediately understand how I blew it:

"I should never have said where I was from," I tell her. "I don't even know, now, why I thought that was important. *Anyone* at this fair, anyone from Kentucky could object to that display."

"Right," Jess, who was born and raised in Massachusetts but has lived in Louisville for eleven years, quickly affirms. "What you did was reinforce every stereotype those people already have. The loud-mouth, know-it-all Yankee who tells 'stupid' southerners what's wrong with them. It might have been better if you hadn't said you were from the North."

Stung by my blunder, I am unable to appreciate the glorious quilts before us. If I can't find a way to say what I am moved to say without making the other person feel defensive or angry or guilty, I might as well keep my mouth shut.

◆

It being a rainy day we continued in our tent, and here I was led to think on the nature of the exercise which hath attended me. Love was the first motion, and then a concern arose to spend some time with the Indians, that I might feel and understand their life and the spirit they live in, if haply I might receive some instruction from them, or they be in any degree helped forward by my following the leadings of Truth amongst them.

—John Woolman, from his Journal

We thought she was another guilty White woman when we first met her: If love were the first motion for John Woolman, guilt was the first for me. Although partially motivated to find Owen Cardwell and Lynda Woodruff by curiosity and then nudged by Spirit to keep moving, it had been my own uneasiness about my adolescent inaction which largely set this leading into motion. Again and again over the past seven years, I have been brought up short by this debilitating emotion, my own, my own kind's, or the guilt I have thoughtlessly produced in others.

To acknowledge the role of guilt in this process is not to diminish the spiritual underpinnings of this leading. Indeed, I believe it was Divine Assistance that allowed me to isolate and to identify this "first motion," it was Divine Assistance which guided me on this journey, and it was Divine Assistance which transformed what had been essentially a selfish motive—"I feel terrible about what I failed to do at seventeen. What can I do to make *myself* feel okay, again?"—into something else: a growing edge, a still-awkward, still-bumpy way to acknowledge, moment by moment, my own privilege.

When I was seventeen, my world was so small, I didn't realize that Prince Edward County was a short car-ride away. Now when I read the morning paper, I rarely need *The Boston Globe*'s helpful maps to pinpoint the latest headline's conflagration or disaster, some, tragically, perpetuated "in my name." "War: How Americans learn geography," someone once noted. How many wars, how many conflicts, how many tragedies, how many geography lessons have been taught during my lifetime! I am a citizen of a troubled world; my guilt is global. What I choose to do with my uneasiness, my piercing awareness of my easeful life while millions suffer seems *the* essential question "for my kind."

As my friend Delia once noted: " 'Why me?' is never the right question whether you're talking about being incredibly blessed or because your life is incredibly difficult." The right question, it seems to me, is contained in Mary Oliver's "The Summer Day": "Tell me, what is it you plan to do/with your one wild and precious life?"

If I have learned nothing else over the past seven years, it has been that guilt itself, when it takes the form of lying awake at 3 a.m. reviewing one's transgressions, is a huge waste of time and energy. A nagging uneasiness with one's self and with the state of the world which, after careful discernment, helps to fuel a leading, however, can be transformational.

✦

Coming home one day on the Red Line, I happened to glance into the next subway car to see a homeless student of mine—let's call her Crystal—pacing back and forth, shouting, sputtering, waving her arms about. A rail-thin African American, always beautifully dressed, her make-up and hair just so, for as long as I had known her, two or three years, now, Crystal would religiously show up for GED classes for a week or two, then disappear. Not hearing from Crystal for months at a time had become so routine, I had stopped worrying about her whereabouts. Her most recent disappearance, however, had gone on far longer than usual and, judging from her behavior in the next subway car, the ensuing months had not been kind.

What to do? Should I get off at the next stop, Porter Square in Cambridge, enter her car, try—although I doubted I knew how—to calm her down? I knew Crystal; did that mean I must assume responsibility here? Am I motivated to do something because, once again, I simply don't want to feel guilty? As I asked myself these questions I remembered hearing that Crystal had been showing up at "On The Rise," a new drop-in center in Porter Square for chronically homeless women. On The Rise had been designed specifically for women like Crystal, homeless women who had been sexually abused as children. There are other caring people in Crystal's life, I reminded myself.

When Crystal indeed got off the train at Porter Square, I prayed that she was heading for On The Rise and its capable staff, women far more able to deal with someone in Crystal's highly agitated state than I.

You must believe that there are other caring and compassionate people in the world, I told myself. To think that you, alone, are responsible for the ills of the world is hubris and a form of spiritual distrust.

✦

In the mysterious way that these things happen, since the summer of 2005, Friends Meeting at Cambridge has been compelled to take a crash course on the plight of returning prisoners. A convergence of circumstances, unbidden yet undeniably present and pressing, have raised deep, challenging, and often painful questions for my faith community: Questions about our inchoate fears, questions about redemption, questions about our willingness to move away from "our comfort zone," questions about how much our race and class and location in an exclusive, prestigious neighborhood inform our decision-making. Our business meeting deliberations are further hampered by the fact that one of our community's most solid and wise and stabilizing voices, Patricia Watson, is gravely ill. We miss her voice, we long for her clarity.

At one of our meetings for business, I find myself on my feet, telling Friends Meeting about the Restoration Jubilee Conference, about Jerry Falwell's and Owen Cardwell's involvement with returning prisoners. As I speak, I again wonder: Could Owen Cardwell, Jerry Falwell, and their conference co-leaders illuminate Friends Meeting at Cambridge's path?

I look around the large, elegantly simple, sun-lit room. No, Patricia Watson is not seated on one of the benches, her head cocked, attentively and prayerfully listening. Others are present at that business meeting, however, men and women I admire and respect, who are actively working on prison issues. Other people from my Meeting faithfully visit prisoners every week, they drive the family members of the incarcerated to visit their loved ones behind bars, they conduct Alternatives to Violence workshops for prisoners, they attend Quaker meetings inside prison, they're lawyers, social workers, yoga instructors, therapists working on criminal justice issues.

You must be the change you wish to see in the world. "You" is a collective noun, I realize, as I take my seat.

NOTES: Changes

p. 172. Yoga practice:
A quote from B. K. S. Iyengar *Yoga: The Path to Holistic Health* has proved helpful:
The person who practices yoga regularly will not become a victim but a master of his or her circumstances and time. The yoga practitioner lives to love and serve the world.

p. 176. "Dummy on order"
Eric and Jess later reported that the replacement tractor-riding dummy was silver!

p. 179. On The Rise
Originally located in Saint John's Episcopal Church in Porter Square, this drop-in center for chronically homeless women has subsequently moved to its own building near Inman Square. I taught creative writing at On The Rise for several years.

pp. 179, 180. Why was Friends Meeting at Cambridge talking about returning prisoners? Precipitating factors included:
The decision in the summer of 2005 to hire an ex-offender to live at our Friends Center to clean and maintain our facilities—and then the decision less than a month later to ask him to leave. This man had not done anything wrong; he was let go because of "liability issues." Both the decision to hire him and the decision to let him go were vociferously debated.

Tom Ash, our Resident Friend, after getting to know someone while visiting him in prison, realized that this prisoner's ability to obtain housing and, therefore, parole were next-to-impossible. Tom felt led to invite this prisoner, if granted parole, to live with him at our Friends Center. Before this leading could be allowed to evolve, however, Tom felt it necessary to withdraw his request because of a fear that sensitive personal information about his friend was not being held carefully within the Meeting community.

A recommendation from Meeting's Personnel Committee to do some kind of criminal background checks on our hired staff elicited a heated discussion on CORIs (the often-confusing system used in Massachusetts to disseminate criminal records), "the Jail Trail," and if and how our meeting wants to perpetuate a system many felt is oppressive.

After months of discussion, sometimes contentious, at its (adjourned) February 25, 2007, business meeting, Friends Meeting grudgingly agreed to conduct criminal background checks on employees and any volunteers working with children. Several people "stood aside," i.e., indicated a willingness to allow the proposal to proceed even though they, themselves, were not in favor of it. Others stated that they felt they could not stand aside.

p. 180. Alternative to Violence Program
For more information: www. avpusa.org

✦

Psalm 42
Though from the Hermons and the springs of Jordan,
And from the hill of Mizar,
Deep calls to deep in the roar of thy cataracts,
And all thy waves, all thy breakers,
Pass over me.

✦

CHAPTER 13
Deep calls to deep

In late October of 2005, Lynda mails me a slim package. Inside I find a DVD and a brief note: "Tell me what you think of this," the always busy college professor writes. Distracted by an unusually hectic fall, Lynda's out-of-the-blue offering sits on my desk for a while. But when I finally get around to watching this DVD, I am immediately hopeful: Could "Til' Justice Rolls Down: The Civil Rights Movement in Lynchburg, Virginia" be a pivotal piece to the What Is God Asking of Me puzzle?

For here is Virgil Wood, elder statesmanlike and reflective, looking back at Lynchburg's civil rights movement and the role he played. Here is Rebecca Owen—so that's what she looked like!—articulating the spiritual underpinnings of her activism. And there are Brenda Hughes Andrews, Owen Cardwell, Jr., Cecelia Jackson, and Lynda Woodruff, seated companionably around a table, all too briefly discussing their harrowing, adolescent experience at E. C. Glass.

"Til' Justice Rolls Down: The Civil Rights Movement in Lynchburg, Virginia" is a half-hour television program researched and produced by Gloria Cannady for Lynchburg's WSET in February 2000, and revised September 23, 2005. Cannady, a childhood friend of Lynda and Owen, lovingly and carefully crafted this compact, comprehensive account, narrated by Dr. Wood. Cannady's DVD also presents fascinating news footage, newspaper headlines, photos, and recordings.

What a powerful teaching and learning tool, I think, putting the DVD back in its case. Could I build on and support this half-hour presentation?

When I propose a study guide *website* for "Til' Justice Rolls Down," Lynda, Owen, and Gloria Cannady immediately and heartily endorse the idea. My keyboard-whiz daughter, Hope, with a degree in computer science, agrees to be the proposed site's web master and to teach her Luddite mother a thing or two about web design. More homework; more to learn. In early April of 2006, Lynchburg's WSET graciously gives permission for the DVD to be used for this educational project.

We're good to go.

✦

"We can't get along until we have an understanding
that we're equals at the table."
—Owen Cardwell

A story told of Cambridge Meeting: Years ago, when our current meeting house was still in the design stage, there was a vigorous debate within our faith community about a fireplace for the proposed new space. Some longed for the warmth, the coziness, the consoling crackle, the hearty smell of a wood fire burning on the hearth. Others, however, worried that the fireplace would become too much of the focus on a Sunday morning when our attention should be on inward matters. After much prayerful consideration, a compromise was reached. Yes, there would be a fireplace. This fireplace would only be visible during the winter months, however. For the remainder of the year, the potential distraction was to be hidden behind a section of paneling which perfectly matched the rest of the wall.

Quakers aren't much for ceremony, representational paraphernalia, ritual, anything that might get in the way of listening to that "still small voice." Yet in 2006, when a few of us from Cambridge Meeting visited the Side-by-Side Community Circle, a program for the formerly incarcerated, we were so deeply moved by what we'd witnessed that we decided to replicate Side-by-Side's ceremony, its ritual, its use of paraphernalia like a "Talking Piece" at Cambridge Meeting.

Held in a fusty church basement in Boston's Jamaica Plain (JP) every Monday evening, the Side-by-Side Community Circle offers a simple meal, a time for announcements about self-help and advocacy programs of particular interest to the formerly incarcerated, and a sharing circle. The number participating varies from Monday to Monday but, generally, ten to fifteen people show up. Some are formerly incarcerated, some work on prison reform and social justice issues, some belong to greater-Boston faith communities. Predominantly, but by no means uniformly, the formerly incarcerated are African American men.

By far the most important part of the evening is the sharing circle which faithfully follows the same prescribed routine: First, Side-by-Side members carefully unroll a large rug a few feet away from where everyone had gathered for the meal and announcements. A suitable number of folding chairs is arranged in a circle around this laid rug. A wrought-iron candelabrum bearing several thick candles is placed in the center of the rug. Whoever assumes responsibility to be the circle's leader that evening lights the candles. The church basement lights are dimmed; everyone takes a seat. The leader reads the Circle's guidelines and values. Someone else lights a bundle of dried sage, places the smoking, fragrant herb on a fireproof dish, then offers this smoky dish to the first seated person. This person cups his or her hands to draw the sage smoke towards him or herself. (This "cleansing ceremony" has been borrowed from a native-American tradition.) The sage bearer performs this ritual with every person until, finally, someone else volunteers to do the same for the bearer. The leader asks each person to make eye contact with everyone seated around the circle, then asks who would like to hold the Talking Piece first.

Side-by-Side's Talking Piece is a sturdy, gnarled stick, maybe four feet tall, burnished by varnish and by the hands of all the people who have held it. As the Circle guidelines make clear, only the person holding the Talking Piece may speak. When that person has finished speaking, the Piece is passed to the next person until everyone who wishes to has been given the opportunity to say something.

What everyone who has attended Side-by-Side will tell you is that, almost always, what is shared around that circle is deep, real, and weighty. As one Prison Fellowship member reported to Cambridge Meeting, "It was very moving to be welcomed into this circle of profound sharing. We found that the program was not so much a service to people who are oppressed and poor—although the formerly incarcerated are usually both—but rather a means of spiritual communion with fellow human beings who are struggling to find our place in society and in God's creation."

During the summer of 2006, five people from Cambridge Meeting, all of us members of the newly-formed Prison Fellowship group at Meeting, took turns attending the JP program. After we'd enthusiastically reported what we'd experienced, Prison Fellowship decided to initiate a meals-and-sharing program at Friends Meeting. The group proposed this idea to the greater-Meeting community in the fall of 2006.

For the rest of that year and the following spring, this proposal was the subject of much discussion at Meeting, both public and private, heated and Spirit-filled. In January of 2007, meeting for worship with attention to business, Cambridge Meeting's decision-making forum, gave the meals-and-sharing program its blessing but requested that Prison Fellowship seek final approval later in the year.

While these intra-Meeting discussions progressed, in anticipation that we'd eventually be given the go-ahead, Prison Fellowship began to set the table: We invited several regulars from Side-by-Side to give us their seasoned advice and under these men's guidance, drafted our own guidelines and a "Circle Values" listing [see Appendix]. Given Quakers' long-held squeamishness over ceremonial paraphernalia, we somewhat self-consciously shopped for just the right candles and a suitable platform or holder to display them. A Somerville neighbor cocked an eyebrow when I explained to her that my Quaker meeting needed dried sage for a cleansing ceremony, but without comment or hesitation supplied an abundant, fragrant bouquet. Tom Ash, Meeting's Resident Friend, and John Field, Meeting's facilities manager, found a suitable rug in the attic of our Friends Center. When Mehmet Rona, a member of Prison Fellowship, offered an exquisite, hand-carved walking stick to be our Talking Piece, his offering was declared perfect by the rest of the group.

"Think of the history this Talking Piece will have," Ron marveled as he held Mehmet's donation one evening. "Think of the stories." One of the Side-by-Side advisors, Ron had continued coming to our meals-and-sharing program—which began, on a contingency basis, in January of 2007. Ron had more to say. Although this Talking Piece was to be used in a brand-new circle, he suggested, the stories told for years in a JP church basement resonated within and transformed our little Cambridge circle, too.

Seated in that darkened Friends Center lit only by soft candlelight, the smell of my neighbor's dried bouquet heavy in the wintry air, I thought about what Ron had just said. His words invited me to contemplate the stories *I* brought to the circle. Like fleeting wisps of candle smoke, stories from my childhood, stories about my daughters, stories my homeless students had confided, many stories, some of them painful to recall, circled and drifted through my mind. Yet what seemed most clear in that sage-scented quiet was that it had been the stories of my leading which bore most directly and so powerfully on that moment: Like the time Lynda had written "CONTEXT!" in the margin of an earlier draft of our book. Her hand-written directive had prompted me to examine Lynchburg's African American history and this country's race relations more deeply. My homework for this leading grounds me, here, I realized in the dark. That homework informs how I now hear the stories told by African Americans. (As in JP, most but not all of the formerly incarcerated people who attend Meeting's program are African American.) I recalled the ex-offender who so movingly spoke at the Restoration Jubilee conference, a conference Owen helped to coordinate: "What I've heard is powerful and poignant," that young woman had shared, tears in her eyes. "It can happen. When I got out, I needed my pastor and my community resources."

The Meeting circle that evening concluded as they always do, by everyone standing, holding hands, and reciting the Serenity Prayer:

> *God grant me the serenity*
> *To accept the things I cannot change,*

The courage to change the things I can,
And the wisdom to know the difference.

"Let go, let God." Those words are often spoken at a sharing circle; I've repeated this simple enjoiner myself. "Let go, let God," I tell myself a dozen times a day. Ironic, isn't it, that so devout a Worshipper of the Written Word should now consider those four, terse syllables to be the center of her life? But I do.

✦

In April of 2007, Friends Meeting at Cambridge approved Prison Fellowship's meals-and-sharing program. Praise Spirit!

NOTES: Deep calls to deep.

p. 18. The website: www.tiljusticerolls.com

p. 186. "It was very moving…"
My husband, David Myers, said this.
Note: More information about FMC's program can be found in the Appendix.

✦

Amos 5:24—Let justice roll on like a river
and righteousness like an ever-flowing stream.

✦

Epilogue

Bubbling in the little pond in Anne Spencer's garden, bursting from the "spring of cool water in a weary land," howling like an overwhelming tsunami, quiet as Lynda's tears when she couldn't find Owen that cold January in 1962, or my own tears when Friends Meeting at Cambridge gave its approval for a meals-and-sharing program: living water.

Swift or sluggish, straight or winding, all rivers end at the sea, salty as tears. Meandering, hesitant, often unclear, I, too, have been drawn towards, moving towards Something as I have followed my leading.

And way has opened.

APPENDIX

Meals and Sharing Circle Program at Friends Meeting at Cambridge

Description:

> *What do we do?* At 6:00 each Friday evening, we gather for a home-cooked meal. After eating, we discuss news, information, and events concerning re-entry from prison, recovery from addiction, and criminal justice reform. About 7:00, we gather for the *Sharing Circle*.

> *What is the Sharing Circle?* The Circle is a time and place where people can speak honestly about what's going on for them. It's a safe, non-threatening forum for each participant to express his or her current concerns, to be listened to patiently and without judgment, and to offer the same in return to others. It's based on mutual respect and equality. It's a simple yet profoundly affirming process in which members hear the truth in one another's statements and lend support as needed.

> *Who comes?* People who have been incarcerated, their families and friends, people in recovery, and anyone interested in being part of a very supportive community.

Details:

1. The meal is cooked by one participant who is paid in advance for food out of money that participants contribute each week (as much as they feel they can, up to $5.00 or so).

2. There is a leader each week who collects contributions, clerks the information session, introduces the sharing circle, and explains things to newcomers. At least two Quakers will be present each week but the leader will not necessarily be a Quaker. Everyone participates on an equal basis otherwise.

3. There are rituals associated with the sharing circle: candlelight, a "talking piece" to indicate who has the floor, burning of sage in a native-American-inspired ceremony. Each participant speaks once for as long as he or she feels a need to (although each participant is encouraged to consider the needs of everyone else). The serenity prayer is recited after a moment of silence at the end of the circle.

4. For the first few weeks, only a handful of people, most of whom have participated in the Jamaica Plain program, will be explicitly invited; the purpose of this is to clearly establish the group's practices and expectations. After that, we will let the group grow slowly. The attendance at the Jamaica Plain program is usually between five and twenty people.

Location: Friends Meeting at Cambridge, 5 Longfellow Park (off Brattle Street about six blocks from Harvard Square). We meet in the building across the driveway from the meeting house itself.

Sharing Circle Guidelines

1. Turn off all cell phones or put them on "vibrate."

2. Respect the Talking Piece; only the person holding it should speak.

3. Speak only from your own personal experience, your own personal feelings and thoughts; use "I" rather than "you" or "they" statements.

4. If addressing individuals, do so respectfully.

5. Refrain from giving advice or opinions.

6. Be mindful of the time when speaking.

7. Commit to remaining in the circle if possible; inform the group at the beginning if you must leave early.

8. Listen attentively and set judgments aside.

9. Maintain confidentiality.

10. Assume responsibility for *everyone's* adherence to these guidelines.

Circle Values

1. Respect for individual human dignity.

2. Equality for all community members.

3. Trust and confidence in the power of community.

4. Mutual responsibility between the individual and the community.

5. Goodwill, support, and healing.

Procedures for the Leader

1. Arrange chairs in a circle around the rug with candles, sage, and lighter in the middle.

2. Light the candles and turn down the lights.

3. Welcome latecomers and newcomers.

4. Read the Circle Guidelines and Circle Values above.

5. Explain that a designated person will light the sage and all participants will have the opportunity to ritually cleanse themselves with the smoke, following a ritual from native-American tradition.

6. Ask for a moment of silence to reflect and gather our thoughts about ourselves in the present moment.

7. Ask participants to look around the room and make eye contact with each person, acknowledging them silently.

8. Initiate the speaking. Ask who would like to take the Talking Piece first to begin the round. Ask participants to pass the stick to the left (clockwise) when they are finished speaking. They need not speak, but ask them to hold the stick for a moment so they can enter our thoughts.

9. After a round, highlight any noteworthy group dynamics and determine whether there is time and inclination for another round.

10. After the last round, allow time for the group to process the session.

11. Stand, join hands, and offer the Serenity Prayer or another closing.

Acknowledgments

Family:

My birth family: Al and Pat Wild, Paul Wild, Deborah Wild Avetissyan, and Ben Wild: Thank you for your love and support, thank you for helping me to better remember our family's time in Lynchburg, thank you for patiently listening when I rattled on and on about the latest bit of Lynchburg history I'd discovered.

My daughters: Melissa Wild-Arons, Hope Roth, Allison Roth, Christina Wild Joanis: How blessed, how grateful, how lucky I am to have four such amazing daughters! Each of you, in ways so reflective of who each of you are, sustained me during this spiritual journey. Thank you.

My husband, David Myers. You've been my L. L. Bean outfitter, my guide and companion every step of the way. How happy I am that you and I will travel the next leg of this trip together!

Jess and Jeremy: Thank you for gracing my life.

To Dick Salwitz, Judy, Tina, and Tyler Wild, Garen and Tiko Avetissyan, Chris and Mike Harris, Dave Arons, Eric Bookstrum, Dustin Ray, Luke Joanis, Kristian Sanchez, and Vita Kaplan: Thank you for all you "bring to the table."

And to my grandson, Dmitri Sol Wild-Arons, who teaches me to consider "the passing on of what I know, what I've experienced to my sphere of influence" in new and powerful ways, thank you.

My Spiritual Community:

Heartfelt thanks to Friends Meeting at Cambridge, especially its Special Sources Fund, its Friends for Racial Justice Committee, and its Witness ad hoc group. How truly grateful I have been over the past seven years, especially in times of confusion and pain, to sit in worship with you all.

Special thanks to FMC's Prison Fellowship group: Jennifer Bills, Maureen and Michael Carey, Chris Connaire, Suzanne Cooper, Barbara Fedders, Lynn Lazar, Diego Low,

Stephanie Messina, Patti Muldoon, Mehmet Rona, Nancy Ruggiero, Michael Shanahan, Sylvia Shurcliff, Gate West. Thank you for the work you're doing. Thank you, too, for your delicious contributions to our monthly potlucks, and the equally nourishing conversations we've had together.

So many FMC individuals have been enormously helpful. In particular, I want to single out Patricia Watson, whose editorial comments on an earlier draft were so enormously illuminating. Much gratitude, too, to Wendy Sanford and Susan Lloyd McGarry for your steadfast encouragement and gentle guidance. Many thanks to my Dream Team: Jonathan Vogel-Borne, Sylvia deMurias, Martha Mangelsdorf, Kitty Rush, Skip Schiel. Much gratitude to Tom Ash, who has been a very special spiritual advisor for me. And much gratitude to Alex Kern, who represents *all* the people at FMC who said just the thing I needed to hear when I was ready to hear it.

My friends:

Special thanks to Delia Marshall, who has, without recompense, edited each draft of this manuscript (and there were so many; I've lost count!), and whose probing questions and wise suggestions have made this a much better book. Remaining errors and lack of clarity are all my fault!

Much gratitude to Polly Attwood, Sharon Boswell, Michele and Darien Brimage, Kathy Bruce, George Capaccio, Brian Corr, Susan Davies, Dolores DeVellis, Gail Fanning-Grove, Lissa Gifford, Ralph Hergert, Doug Holder, Joanne Holdridge, Christel Jorgenson, Alison Keehn, Anne Kriebel, Brian Kuhl, Donna McDaniel, Melissa McWhinney, Bunny Meyer, Jan Nisenbaum, Buzzy Olan, Byron Parrish, Harriet Rapson, Ellen Rauch, Emily Sander, Nancy Sowell, Andrew Szanton, Jane Trevithick, Janie Warren, Lynne Weiss, Cathy Whitmire, Lynn Wiles, and Susan Zeichner; the Jehlens and the Grunkos and the Bonner-Jacksons: each and every one of you contributed to this effort. Thank you.

Lynchburg people:

Brenda Hughes Andrews, Ed and Georgia Barksdale, Carolyn Bell, Susan Bunch Blanchard, Jane Barringer Bowen, Dr. Leslie M. Camm, Gloria Cannady, W. E. Clark III, Gill Cobbs, Ted Delaney, Henry Faulkner Heil, Cecilia Jackson, Bishop Alfred Kee, Darrell and Gail Laurant, Nancy Marion, Susan Morrison, Jim Owens, Bill Ramsey, Sherry Scruggs, Chauncey and Anne Spencer, Susan White, Dr. Virgil Wood; thank you for your time, your stories, your help, your wealth of information, your support.

Joyce Maddox has been an extraordinary resource throughout the correction and revision process. Numerous times I'd come upon one of her red-inked changes in the manuscript margin and say aloud: "Praise Spirit she caught that!"

Of course, if it hadn't been for the courageous, extraordinary Owen Cardwell and Lynda Woodruff, this journey would not have happened. Thank you for trusting me, thank you for your candor, your wisdom, your friendship.

Research help:

Many thanks to the patient and hard-working staff at the Somerville Public Library, especially the research librarians. Thanks, too, to the staff at Harvard University's Harvard College Library for letting me read their African American newspapers on microfilm (and for Carla Lillvik's help to print what I needed!). I am grateful for the help given by the reference librarians at Lynchburg's Jones Memorial Library and the staff at the Legacy Museum.

Thanks, too, to Marian Anderson Jones for her invaluable help.

Many thanks to the students who attended and ran the Cambridge Rindge and Latin School Race Forum (especially the young man in the Malcolm X tee shirt), Joseph Burke and the history teachers and students at Somerville High School, and the E. C. Glass students who gave Lynda and Owen that standing O.

And finally, many thanks to the folks at the JP meals and sharing program, especially Bob David, Ron Owens, KT, Kevin, and George.

134, 141
52, ANNE SPENCER, Harlem Renssnce poet
65 Jerry Falwell (& earlier), 71,
82 Isaac Penington
100,1 a' little cousin's) comment
101+ 9/11/01
116 "9 [PW] ventured there every wk" - (volntr?)
118 Black Like Me Joshua Solomon 1994
    White "   " Tim Wise
119 see Lazarus book ref, at end
141 pyred - ?
148 Susan McGarry's "Empire"
160 Howard Levy's "Jackson, MS, 1966"